Your Saved Bro.
D. S. Warner

SALVATION,

PRESENT, PERFECT, NOW OR NEVER.

By D. S. WARNER.

GOSPEL TRUMPET PUBLISHING CO.
MOUNDSVILLE, W. VA.

Biographical Sketch.

THE subject of this sketch was born in Bristol, Wayne Co., Ohio, on the 25th of June, 1843. From his birth his life was one of sorrow, pain, and suffering. The enemy of all truth seemed to foresee that God intended to use him as one of his chief instruments in establishing a great reformation in the world, by which thousands of precious souls who were bound in the chains of darkness might be led out into the beautiful Evening Light and set free. Therefore the archfiend put forth his best efforts to destroy his life, beginning as soon as he was born.

The following beautiful lines penned by his own hand, show the disadvantages under which he labored in early life.

> Conceived in sin, to sorrow born,
>   Unwelcome here on earth,
> The shadows of a life forlorn,
>   Hung gloomy o'er my birth.
>
> A mother's heart oppressed with grief,
>   A father's wicked spleen,
> Who cursed my faint and gasping breath,
>   Combine to paint the scene.
>
> But life held on its tender thread,
>   Days unexpected grew
> To weeks, and still he lived,
>   Why, heaven only knew.
>
> He lived, though life was bitter gain,
>   His youth a flood of tears,
> His body doomed to creul pain,
>   His mind to nervous fears."

But the heavenly Father had his eye upon him and sent his guardian angel to protect his tender years. He was converted when about twenty-two years of age, and a few weeks afterward enlisted as a soldier in the Union Army, and went to fight for his country. It is said that he did this to save his brother, who was a man of a family, and about to be drafted, going in his stead and acting as his substitute. He remained a short time and returned home. About two years after his conversion he entered upon the duties of a minister of the gospel, and in this capacity he labored faithfully with tongue and pen until the close of his life.

During his early Christian experience the Lord began to show him the true church, the body of Christ; but the light not being clear, he was influenced by certain parties to unite with the so-called Church of God, or Winebrennarians. He was deceived in making this step because of their name "Church of God," which he well knew by the Word was correct; and not discerning, clearly the body of Christ he yielded to their solicitations.

He remained in this sect about ten years, but never enjoyed the spiritual liberty and freedom he had before uniting with this body. In the year 1879 he became interested in a paper called the *"Herald of Gospel Freedom,"* which was published in the interest of the sect to which he belonged, acting as the editor of the holiness department. In the year 1880, he became editor of the whole paper, and during this prophetic year God showed him more clearly than ever before the evils of sectism, the downfall of Babylon, and enabled him to discern the body of Christ, the true church. True to his convictions of right, he at once began to cry out against sectism, proving by the Word that she is a part of Babylon, and exhorting God's little ones to come out of her that they partake not of her plagues.

This astounding declaration fell like a thunderbolt from heaven (which it was) on the sectarian world, and it appeared that all the demons of earth and hell were stirred, and they became terribly enraged against him. He was persecuted, tried, afflicted and tormented; but God's grace was sufficient and enabled him to stand for the truth. After having assumed control of the paper mentioned, he became impressed that its name ought to be changed, and he laid the matter before God, asking what it should be called. "GOSPEL TRUMPET," came ringing in his soul. This was the name he got from heaven, and this name is no doubt destined to become familiar with God's children throughout the length and breadth of the earth.

After removing a number of times from place to place he finally settled permanently at Grand Junction, Mich., where the paper is still published. He was very earnest and zealous in his work for the Master. Although his body was frail and his constitution weak from the day of his birth, yet by the help of the Lord, he was enabled to accomplish a vast amount of work during his life. He seemed to be a living miracle, and it can be truly said that he walked and labored in the strength of God. He is the author of a number of books including one of poems which will probably be reissued in a revised and enlarged form. The following is a copy of the last poem he was engaged in writing, just before the summons came, calling him away, leaving it unfinished. The first stanza, two lines of the chorus, and one line of the second stanza, is all that was written. It is entitled

A HYMN.

Shall my soul ascend with rapture,
  When the day of life is past?
While my house of clay shall slumber,
  Shall I then with Jesus rest?

Cho.—O my soul, press on to glory!
    Worlds of bliss invite thee on.

O shall my immortal spirit,

We see in this that his thoughts were being wafted
away to his future and eternal home, to which he was
so soon to be called. He was sick but a few days with
an affection of the lungs and heart, and God gave him
grace to bear his sufferings very patiently, when on the
morning of Dec. 12th, 1895, about 3 A. M. he quietly and
gently passed away.

SALVATION.

1st. SALVATION—WHAT DOES IT MEAN?

O reader, have you given attention to that which is contained in the word SALVATION? O man, think of this; it concerns you more than all other objects taken together for which the whole world is in pursuit.

Salvation is worth a thousand times more than health of body; in comparison with which men consider money no object; and for the hope of regaining they lavish gold and greenbacks as free as dirt.

. Salvation is more to be desired than all the glory and pleasure that the highest honors of earth can yield. Yea, it places the soul upon a plane so elevated as to receive the admiration and adoration of Heaven. "If any man serve me, saith the Lord, him will my Father honor." —Jno. 12: 26. It places a man far above the highest object of earthly ambition. It gives him a kingdom greater than Alexander or Napoleon ever swayed scepter over. "It is your Father's good pleasure to give you the kingdom." Even the "kingdom of heaven." "They which receive abundance of grace and the gift of righteousness, shall reign in life by one Jesus Christ."—Rom. 5: 17. And this glorious reign is not located in some future age; but John, writing to the seven churches in Asia, in the first century of Christian grace, declared that Jesus Christ, who is the faithful Witness, the Prince of the kings of the earth, him that loved us, and washed us from our sins in his own blood, hath also "made us kings and priests unto God and his Father."—Rev. 1: 5, 6. As again seen in this beautiful book of symbols, at the very opening of the plan of redemption the blood-washed celebrated the praises of God with a "new song, saying, Thou art worthy to take the book, and to open the seals thereof: for thou wast slain, and hast redeemed us to God by thy blood, out of every kindred, and tongue, and people, and nation; and hast made us unto our God kings and priests, and we shall reign on the earth."—Rev. 5: 9, 10. And Peter calls God's church "a royal priesthood," *i. e.*, a priesthood of kings.

All who live in sin are slaves to their own
lusts, and are not able to govern themselves.
But salvation makes us kings in rule over our
own selves; over our passions, appetites and
desires. "And he that ruleth his spirit is greater
than he that taketh a city."—Prov. 16: 32. Salvation also places us in kingly triumph over all
the elements of this world; over sin, fashion,
and popular sentiments; and over the devil
himself, who claims to be the ruler of earth. A
master of the situation of life, with a peace that
nothing disturbs; and a joyful faith in God
which sees all things working together for our
good, and contributing to our happiness.

Salvation is greater riches than all the gold,
silver and valuable treasures of this earth sum-
med up together. A treasure that never faileth;
a wealth so great that to the happy possessor
every thing of earth is, in comparison, reduced
to dust and dirt. O "the unsearchable riches of
Christ!" Eph. 3: 8. "Ye know the grace of
our Lord Jesus Christ, that though he was rich,
yet for your sakes he became poor, that ye
through his poverty might be rich."—2 Cor. 8: 9.
How rich? "He that overcometh shall inherit
all things."—Rev. 21: 7. "He that spared not
his own Son, but delivered him up for us all,

how shall he not with him also freely give us all
things?"—Rom. 8: 32. Yea, hath given. "For
all things are yours. Whether Paul or Apollos,
or Cephas, or the world, or life, or death, or
things present, or things to come, all are yours."
—1 Cor. 3: 22.

So teaches the word of God, and so bear
witness all who have tested its wonderful claims.
Reader, look back over that long line of holy
martyrs, who, in the possession of this great
treasure, gloried in tribulations, and shouted for
joy amid the flames; disdaining life, with all it
could offer, when tendered to them as a com-
pensation for their hope in Christ; and there
behold the eternal and incalculable value of
salvation. If, then, such unbounded wealth,
such innumerable blessings, and such infinite
bliss and happiness are all treasured up in SAL-
VATION, who can afford to be indifferent to the
gracious treasure? But again we ask, What
does it mean?

2d. SALVATION MEANS DELIVERANCE.

The entrance of sin into our world has brought
in its train indescribable wretchedness. Guilt

and remorse sting the conscience and fill the soul with shame. Sinful habits form the links of an iron chain, which binds the life in utter despair. A chain of bondage which defies all human strength. Burning lusts are set on fire from hell, all clamoring for unholy indulgence; the gratification of which is only followed by greater misery. Restless and unnatural desires deprive the soul of peace; and the half-awakened fears of death and judgment hang dark and gloomy over the life. Hope dies, and with it, manhood and womanhood give up their struggle, and surrender the life to dark melancholy or open shame. Reader, SALVATION MEANS DELIVERANCE from all these elements of woe and misery. And should even this picture fall short of the deep shades of your case, SALVATION yet means complete deliverance for you. Actual deliverance from the strongest chains of habit, the lowest depths of sin, the deepest hell of intemperance and debauchery. Deliverance from darkness into light, from the power of Satan unto God. From the woes of a guilty conscience into peace with God through our Lord Jesus Christ; from remorse into the joys of pardon; from the thralldom of sin into the glorious liberty of the sons of God. O how wonderful! wonderful!! deliverance by the almighty arm of Him whose name is Wonderful!

And when all this blessedness is reached by the divine miracle of regeneration, if the new-born soul continues to "desire the sincere milk of the Word, and grow thereby," he will soon come to the privilege of another great and glorious epoch in divine grace; the entire sanctification of his nature; the utter destruction of all inward bent to evil, and the restoration of the "divine nature." 2 Pet. 1: 4. Perfect deliverance from the "body of sin," into the "image of God," and his perfected love.

Beloved, this is not an overdrawn picture, nor a tale of human fancy. Nay, it is the very substance of the sure word of God. "For he hath made him to be sin for us, who knew no sin; that we might be made the righteousness of God in him."—2 Cor. 5: 21.

"Wherefore he is able also to save them to the uttermost that come unto God by him, seeing he ever liveth to make intercession for them."—Heb. 7: 25.

"This is a faithful saying, and worthy of all acceptation, that Jesus Christ came into the world to save sinners; of whom I am chief."— 1 Tim. 1: 15.

And "where sin abounded grace did much more abound."—Rom. 5: 20.

Here saving grace is placed over against all sin. And even in hearts and lives where "sin abounded," grace, the saving mercy of God, much more abounds. Though your sins tower up like dark mountains unto heaven, grace towers far above. Though they be as deep as hell, the grace of God with omnipotent arm reaches unto you. Though great wickedness spreads over all your past life, grace superabounds to save you. Though your sins be as scarlet, they shall be as white as snow; though they be red like crimson, they shall be as wool." —Isa. 1: 18.

If we confess our sins, he is faithful and just to forgive us our sins, and to cleanse us from all unrighteousness."—1 John 1: 9. "And the blood of Jesus Christ, his Son, cleanseth us from all sin."—1 John 1: 7. To meet your wants as a great sinner, God has sent to you "a Savior and a great one." Isa. 19: 20. Though your soul is cursed by your manifold transgressions, and your *mighty sins*," Amos 5: 12, you may "make your *supplication to the Almighty*."—Job 8: 5. "Though your lusts and wickedness rise like mighty billows and threaten to sweep you quickly down to hell, "The Lord on high is mightier than the noise of many waters, yea, than the mighty waves of the sea."—Psa. 93: 4.

"And being made perfect he became the author of eternal salvation to all them that obey him."—Heb. 5: 9.

"For if the blood of bulls and of goats, and the ashes of a heifer sprinkling the unclean, sanctifieth to the purifying of the flesh; how much more shall the blood of Christ, who through the eternal Spirit offered himself without spot to God, purge your conscience from dead works to serve the living God?"—Heb. 9: 13, 14.

Reader, be assured that the writer is one, and he is personally acquainted with thousands of others, who, though our case has been as dark and hopeless as yours, have, by the grace of God come to a happy realization of those precious scriptures. Therefore, *full salvation* is not only true in the Word, but also in fact. And if you are willing and obedient will prove true in your case.

3d. SALVATION MAKES US FREE FROM SIN.

"For he that is dead is free from sin. Now if we be dead with Christ we believe we shall also live with him."—Rom. 6: 7, 8.

"For in that he died, he died unto sin once; but in that he liveth, he liveth unto God. Likewise reckon ye also yourselves to be dead indeed unto sin, but alive unto God through Jesus Christ our Lord."—Rom. 6: 10, 11.

"Being then made free from sin, ye became the servants of righteousness."—Rom. 6: 18.

"He that is dead is free from sin." And this freedom is attained now in this life. Hence immediately follow the words, "Now if we be dead with him," etc. And just as Christ lives unto God, a holy life, "likewise, in the same manner we should reckon ourselves dead indeed unto sin, but alive unto God through Jesus Christ our Lord." Not dead to sin prospectively, or only professedly, but DEAD INDEED UNTO SIN. Actually dead and oblivious to sin. Having no more part in the sins of this world than if literally dead and buried. What can more strongly and more positively express absolute freedom from sin than the declaration that we are dead indeed to sin? One might abstain from the commission of sin and yet not be really dead to it. But when dead indeed to any thing that must be the end of it. It means that we have no more to do with sin than the dead who lay in the cemetery have to do with the business of this world. As natural death puts an end to all activities here on earth, so complete salvation in Jesus is the terminus of all human actions of a sinful character.

"But now being made free from sin, and become servants to God, ye have your fruit unto holiness, and the end everlasting life."—Rom. 6: 22.

4th. SALVATION KEEPS US FROM COMMITTING SINS.

"Knowing this, that our old man is crucified with him, that the body of sin might be destroyed, that henceforth we should not serve sin."—Rom. 6: 6.

Men's outward lives are usually an expression of their inward state. Therefore, the condition of being free from sin will naturally exclude sin from the outward life. As certain as a pure fountain will send forth a pure stream, from a pure heart there will proceed a holy life. For "out of the abundance of the heart the mouth speaketh," and all moral actions flow. Out of the heart, we are told, "are the issues of life."

But do the Scriptures actually teach that salvation enables us to live without committing sins? There are a few texts in the Old and New Testaments which, when not rightly understood, seem to teach the contrary. One of these is in Solomon's dedicatory prayer, 1 Kings 8: 46; a parenthesis reading as follows, "For there is no man that sinneth not." A very sensible translation of these words is found in the version of the Old Testament by Isaac Leeser, a Jew. It reads as follows: "If they sin against thee (for there is no man that may not sin"). Here is a beautiful consistency that is wanting in the Common version, which reads as follows: "If they sin against thee (for there is no man that sinneth not"). In the use of the word "if," a mere possibility of their sinning is expressed, while a probability remains that they may not sin. But the next clause virtually asserts that there is no if about it, that all men do sin. There is, therefore, a lameness in the translation that must be apparent to all. A direct disagreement between the two parts of the same verse. But as rendered by Leeser the verse is consistent with itself and with the Bible through-

2

out. It does not teach that all men must and
do commit sin; but all may sin. And so may
angels in heaven sin. And some have "sinned,"
and "kept not their first estate," "but left their
own habitation."—2 Pet. 2: 4. Jude 6. While
all intelligent volitional creatures of God may
sin, there is no necessity for any child of God
on earth to commit sin. But there are in Christ
Jesus abundant supplies of grace whereby all
may very easily live free from sin.

We will not here take up other texts that are
supposed to teach that we must all continue to
be sinners in this life. They are all explained
in a tract entitled, "Must We Sin?" found in our
catalogue. But let us appeal to the Scriptures
to find our privileges in Christ. While the Bible
draws the true picture of human depravity, the
universal sinfulness of our race, aside from the
grace of God, it also teaches the all sufficiency
of salvation to preserve us from the being and
practice of sin. Anything less would not be
salvation. "Thou shalt call his name JESUS, for
he shall save his people from their sins."—
Matt. 1: 21. Jesus means Savior. If he is not
able to save and keep us from all sin he is not
correctly named. We are told that Zacharias
was filled with the Holy Spirit, and prophesied,

saying, "Blessed be the Lord God of Israel; for
he hath visited and redeemed his people, and
hath raised up a horn of salvation for us in the
house of his servant David."—Luke 1:68, 69.

"To perform the mercy promised to our fa-
thers, and to remember his holy covenant; the
oath which he sware to our father Abraham,
that he would grant unto us, that we, being
delivered out of the hand of our enemies, might
serve him without fear, in holiness and righteousness before him, all the days of our life."
—Verses 72–75.

Salvation in Christ does not leave us to re-
sume the life of sinning in a modified degree, as
too many in error teach, not knowing the Scriptures nor the power of God. Nay, the Lord has
indeed "visited and redeemed his people;" "delivered us out of the hands of our enemies;" all
inward foes that prone the heart to leave the
God we love. And the result of this deliverance
is that we may "serve God without fear in holiness and righteousness before him all the days
of our life." And no person can live a life of
sinning and holiness at the same time. Jesus
has settled this question when he answered that
"no man can serve two masters." And again,
"He that sinneth is the servant of sin." There-

fore is not the servant of the Lord. "A good tree cannot bring forth evil fruit, nor an evil tree good fruit." Therefore he whose life brings forth sin, is a sinner and not a Christian.

To the man that Jesus healed at the pool of Bethesda he said, "Behold, thou art made whole: sin no more, lest a worse thing come unto thee." —John 5: 14. Thirty and eight years this poor man had been bound by a great affliction. Would the Lord Jesus heal and forgive him, and then threaten him with a greater calamity in case he sinned again, were it impossible to abstain from sinning? This were cruelty instead of a blessing.

To the woman Jesus pardoned of her many sins he said, "Go and sin no more."—Jno. 8: 11. Who but a cruel tyrant would exact of his subjects a thing impossible? But such is not the character of Him that issued the imperative prohibition, "Sin not."

The Apostle Paul, writing to the Corinthians, says, "I fear, lest when I come, I shall not find you such as I would, and that I shall be found unto you such as ye would not." "Lest when I come again, my God will humble me among you, and that I shall bewail many which have sinned already."—2 Cor. 12: 20, 21.

To him, sin, in the realm of professed Christianity was a shocking thing. Instead of expecting them to sin, his righteous soul was stirred with holy indignation because many of them had sinned. He bewailed the fact and threatened to come unto them with the scourge of sharp rebukes. He had surely taught them something better than the modern sinnership religion; hence his surprise that "many had sinned." But these words also prove that even in that carnal congregation all had not been guilty of sinning. Therefore, none need to have been.

Hear this solemn blast from the trump of God: "Awake to righteousness and sin not; for some have not the knowledge of God; I speak this to your shame."—1 Cor. 15: 34. The man that sins is here represented as being asleep in sin, and ignorant of God; a condition in which it is a shame in the sight of God for any man to be, more especially if professing Christ. He, therefore, that sins is not a Christian; not even awake unto righteousness.

Jesus tells us (Luke 15: 7), "Joy shall be in heaven over one sinner that repenteth, more than over ninety and nine just persons, which need no repentance." Reader, do you know why a just person needs no repentance? If not, let David inform you, in Psa. 119: 1, 3: "Blessed are the undefiled in the way, who walk in the law of the Lord." "*They also do no iniquity;* they walk in his ways." The Apostle John also gives you a good reason for the same thing: "Whosoever abideth in him, sinneth not: whosoever sinneth hath not seen him neither known him." —1 John 3: 6. No wonder God's children need no repentance; they do no iniquity; they "sin not." This is a fact so fundamental in the divine life, that upon it the inspired apostle bases the chief distinction between the children of God and the chilren of the devil. "He that committeth sin is of the devil;" and "Whosoever is born of God doth not commit sin; for his seed remaineth in him; and he cannot sin because he is born of God." In this, the children of God are manifest, and the children of the devil."—1 John 3: 8-10. Is not this plain Bible truth? The children of the devil sin. The children of God do not sin; and by these facts each class is made manifest to the eyes of all men. Here is the dividing line between the family of God and the kingdom of Satan. Which side are you on? God authorizes all men to classify you with the world if you commit sin. John repeats again in this epistle (5:18), in the following positive terms: *"We know* that whosoever is born of God sinneth not, but he that is begotten of God keepeth himself, and that wicked one toucheth him not."

What can modern teachers, who confess they sin daily in word, thought and deed, do with these scriptures? Some tell us that he that is born of God cannot avoid sinning because in this wicked world. But thus saith the Lord: "Whatsoever is born of God overcometh the world."—1 John 5:4. If, therefore, the world overcomes you, you are not born of God. Others tell us that he that is born of God does not sin habitually, or does not commit great, or mortal sins. But over against these theories stand the words of God: "Whosoever is born of God doth not commit sin." "Whosoever abideth in him sinneth not." Does not sin at all but keepeth himself. It is very humiliating for pampered members of the worldly sects to confess they are yet in the devil's family. But in every attempt to deny that fact while they yet practice sin, the immutable word of God stares them in the face, contradicts their profession, and overthrows their dead hope. Dear reader, we pray you to soberly think of this matter. How can you rest at ease with the word of God directly against you? If it stands, you cannot stand when judged by it in the last day. If you sin, you know just where God classifies you.

"My little children, these things write I unto you, that ye sin not."–1 Jno. 2:1. What utter darkness and confusion to suppose John would write these young converts for the purpose of instructing them, in the grace of God, that they sin not, and in the same epistle say, as some imagine he does, "If any man saith he liveth and sinneth not, he is a liar," etc. Thousands go on consoling themselves with this home-made scripture, living in sin, and yet hope to get to heaven. But salvation makes us free from sin, and puts an end to the business of sinning; and without this salvation your soul is lost forever.

———▸•◂———

5th. SALVATION FITS US TO LIVE HOLY IN THIS LIFE.

———

"For the grace of God that bringeth salvation hath appeared to all men, teaching us that, denying ungodliness and worldly lusts, we should live soberly, righteously, and godly, in this present world; looking for that blessed hope, and the glorious appearing of the great God and our Saviour Jesus Christ; who gave himself for us, that he might redeem us from all iniquity, and purify unto himself a peculiar people, zealous of good works." Titus 2:11–14. Here is a whole sermon. Salvation is not the result of our good works; but the outflow of God's grace, the pure gift of his mercy. It is not reserved in heaven for us, but has appeared on earth to all men, and is delivered free of charges at the door of every heart. It redeems us from all iniquity. It teaches us how to deny ungodliness and worldly lusts. Namely, it gives us power to fully abstain from all sin, and say no to every presentation of evil. And as a result we live soberly, righteously and godly in this present world.

We have already seen—Luke 1—that the covenant of divine mercy provides grace whereby we may serve God without fear in righteousness and true holiness before him all the days of our life.

"There is therefore now no condemnation to them which are in Christ Jesus, who walk not after the flesh, but after the Spirit. For the law of the Spirit of life in Christ Jesus hath made me free from the law of sin and death."–Rom. 8:1, 2.

"I am crucified with Christ: nevertheless I live; yet not I, but Christ liveth in me: and the life which I now live in the flesh I live by the faith of the Son of God, who loved me, and gave himself for me."—Gal. 2:20.

"For to me to live is Christ, and to die is gain."—Phil. 1:21. His spiritual life was purely the life of Christ in him; and in all its minutia redounded to the glory of God.

"Who his own self bare our sins in his own body on the tree, that we being dead to sins, should live unto righteousness; by whose stripes ye were healed."—1 Pet. 2:24. These testimonies are descriptive of God's will in us, and our privileges in Christ. For the same salvation which the apostles enjoyed we need, and the same Christ who saved them from all sin is able to do the same for us. Nor is there any respect of persons with God. If, therefore, the apostles and first disciples of Christ attained an experience where they were really "crucified with Christ," "dead to sin," and "free from sin," and their life was simply the Christ life in them, God requires the same of us all. While the gifts of God in salvation are various, salvation itself is the same to all. And we all need the same holiness of heart to fill our calling in life, how-

ever humble it may be; and to fit us for heaven.
Therefore he who testified to the Roman brethren that "the Spirit of life in Christ Jesus had
made him free from the law of sin and death,"
also tells them, and us as well, "to reckon themselves dead indeed unto sin." He who said to
the Galatians, "I am crucified," etc. also commands them, saying, "Walk in the Spirit and ye
shall not fulfill the lusts of the flesh." "And
they—the children of God—that are Christ's—
fully given to him—have crucified the flesh, with
the affections and lusts." He who told the Ephe-
sians that God had chosen us in Christ even
"before the foundation of the world, that we
should be holy, and without blame before him
in love,"—1: 4, commanded them to "put off,
concerning the former conversation, the old
man which is corrupt according to the deceitful
lusts; and be renewed in the Spirit of your
mind; and that ye put on the new man, which
after God is created in righteousness and true
holiness."—4: 22–24. Thus we might go through
all the Epistles and find that the highest plane
of salvation and holiness gained by the apostles
is also administered to and enjoined upon all
the children of God.

6th. SALVATION TWOFOLD.

There is a late creed comprising what is called "The Fourfold Gospel." But since we read of nothing of the kind in the old Bible, we may safely conclude that this is "another gospel," a new arrangement. If we go beyond the oft expressed twofold salvation of the Word, we see no propriety in summing up the gospel in four special gifts, since its divine mercies are, we may safely say, a thousand fold, its blessings innumerable. But the great object of the Saviour's death is to save men from all sin. And because sin exists in two forms, the word of God often presents salvation as a twofold remedy for sin. And, following the Word in this simple classification of its saving power, we of course for the time being, confine ourselves to the Scriptural method of deliverance from all unrighteousness, without reference to the many other precious gifts of divine grace that accompany salvation.

We have said that sin exists in two distinct forms. The first is the actual commission of sins. All understand that every willful act of disobedience to God's word is sin. Hence it is written, "Sin is the transgression of the law."

1 John 3:4. But again it is written, "All unrighteousness is sin." 1 John 5:17. Therefore if there is such a thing as an unrighteous nature in fallen humanity, it is sin. That is sin in nature; sin as a moral element, or bent to evil, back of, and distinct from all sinful actions that arise from it. This is a fact clearly taught in the Scriptures, and consciously experienced in all unsanctified humanity. It is said to be "sin that dwelleth in me." Rom. 7:17. Sin in "motion." Ver. 5. "Sin working death in me." Ver. 13. Thus we see that sin exists as an element of moral evil; as an indwelling, moving, working force. The same is also called the "body of sin," "the old man." Rom. 6:6. It is also denominated the "works of the devil." 1 John 3:8. This foe to the human soul is infused in man's fallen nature. Eph. 2:3. And is hereditary from the fall of our race. Psa. 51:5–7.

To meet and remove this twofold form of sin the Bible sets before us a double remedy. It is anticipated in the Old Testament. Thus saith the evangelistic prophet Isaiah, 61:6, 7, "Ye shall eat the riches of the Gentiles, and in their glory ye shall feast yourselves. For your shame ye shall have *double*; and for confusion they shall rejoice in their portion: therefore in their land they shall *possess the double:* everlasting joy shall be unto them."

Thus when the Gentiles were brought into the fold of Christ, in the present more glorious dispensation, the promise is that instead of our sins we should "possess the double,"—double salvation imparting everlasting joy. Thank God for a twofold salvation, removing both sins committed, and sin inherited. A double measure of divine grace, which saves to the uttermost from all kinds of sins, and sin.

Looking forward to the Gospel era, it is said, "In that day there shall be a fountain opened to the house of David and to the inhabitants of Jerusalem for sin, and uncleanness."—Zech. 13:1. Namely, to remit sins and cleanse out indwelling unrighteousness.

In Isa. 26:3, we read, "Thou wilt keep him in perfect peace, whose mind is stayed on thee: because he trusteth in thee." But instead of "perfect peace," the marginal reading is "peace, peace." So also in Young's Translation. This is prophetic of the twofold grace in its present reign of Christ. Accordingly we open the New Testament and we read that justification gives us *"peace with God."* Rom 5:1. We also read that *"The peace of God,* which passeth all understanding, shall keep your hearts and minds through Christ Jesus."—Phil. 4:7. The former implies a surrender to God, and reconciliation to the divine will, which comes through repentance, and is in justification. The second, "the peace of God," comes through perfect consecration to God, and consists in the holiness of God. The perfect tranquillity that reigns in a heart that is pure even as Christ is pure. So we have peace —peace. Peace with God, and the holy peace of God.

"Therefore being justified by faith, we have peace with God through our Lord Jesus Christ; by whom also we have access by faith into this grace wherein we stand, and rejoice in hope of the glory of God."—Rom. 5:1, 2.

Here are clearly taught two successive accesses through Christ: first into justification; second, into the standing, or stablishing grace; which is perfect heart holiness. See 1 Thess. 3:13. And each time it is distinctly said that we enter by faith. Therefore the second grace, as well as justification the first, is not a growth, a development of the first, nor by works, and indeed, by no gradual process, but, being by faith, it is grasped as an instantaneous gift from God, purifying the heart by faith.

In the first chapter to the Romans, the apostle expresses his solicitude for the advancement of the church to the possession of this perfected salvation, says he longed to see them and impart unto them the precious "spiritual gift" that establishes the soul. Ver. 11. And this he proposed to do by preaching unto them the "gospel of Christ which is the power of God unto salvation to every one that believeth. For therein is the righteousness of God revealed *from faith to faith*."—Ver. 16, 17. From the first plane of faith to the fulness.

Christ promised the church a fulness of joy. John 15:11. And John thus testifies concerning that grace: "And of his fulness have we all received, and *grace for grace*."—John 1:16. The preposition "for" has the force of either because of or in order to. If we give it the former application, this text teaches a measure of divine grace received because of a former experience in grace. If the latter, it shows a cardinal grace in order to the reception of the fulness. So it matters not which way we take it.

In exact harmony with this process of salvation, Paul writes to Titus, saying, "Not by works of righteousness which we have done, but according to his mercy he saved us, by the

washing of regeneration, and the renewing of
the Holy Spirit; which he shed on us abundantly through Jesus Christ our Saviour."—Tit.
3:5, 6. This, it would seem, is too plain to need
comment. Salvation is in two measures; first,
regeneration, second, the renewal—of the soul
in the divine image, see Col. 3:10,—by the sanc-
tifying power of the Holy Spirit.

The double cure for sin is also seen in 1 John
1:9: "If we confess our sins, he is faithful and
just to forgive us our sins, and to cleanse us
from all unrighteousness." This is a very precious and comprehensive truth. It assures of
pardon, first, then on the same condition of confessing our state, we receive the perfecting grace
of God which sweeps out of our nature all
unrighteousness. That must necessarily include
inbred unrighteousness. This glorious gospel,
we are happy to testify is true. Praise the
name of Jesus! We will conclude by introduc-
ing one more of the precious couplets that des-
cribe the twofold salvation of the Bible.

"But we all, with open face beholding as in a
glass the glory of the Lord, are changed into
the same image from glory to glory, *even* as by
the Spirit of the Lord."—2 Cor. 3:18.

By the wonderful saving and transforming

grace of God we are changed from our sinful
state into the very image of God, yea, into the
image of the glory of the Lord. But this wonderful change is not wrought by a single touch of
divine power. First we must be raised from guilt
and shame, into the precious glory of justification; and from that degree of glory we are
changed into the fulness of glory, into the very
image of the glory of the Lord. ·And, observe,
this glory of the image of the Lord is not received by a transition from earth to heaven, but
it is by the Spirit of the Lord. And he is the
sanctifier. Rom. 15:16.

So, dear reader, if you have been born of God,
and your soul is yet thirsting and longing for
"more grace," that is just what God wants to
give you. Jas. 4:6. Therefore consecrate your
all forevermore to God, and on the authority of
his Word believe the very God of peace sanctifies you wholly, through the precious blood of
his Son, and it shall be done. Amen.

7th. SALVATION MAKES US PERFECT.

It is a very common utterance in the camp of formality that no one may hope to be perfect in this life. But what says the Word?

1. *Perfection is commanded* both in the Old and New Testaments.

"And when Abram was ninety years old and nine, the Lord appeared to Abram, and said unto him, I am the Almighty God; walk before me, and be thou perfect."—Gen. 17:1.

"Thou shalt be perfect with the Lord thy God."—Deut. 18:13.

"And thou, Solomon my son, know thou the God of thy father, and serve him with a perfect heart and with a willing mind: for the Lord searcheth all hearts, and understandeth all the imaginations of the thoughts: if thou seek him, he will be found of thee; but if thou forsake him, he will cast thee off for ever."—1 Chron. 28:9.

"Be ye therefore perfect, even as your Father which is in heaven is perfect."—Matt. 5:48.

"The disciple is not above his master: but every one that is perfect shall be as his master." —Luke 6:40.

"Having therefore these promises, dearly beloved, let us cleanse ourselves from all filthiness of the flesh and spirit, perfecting holiness in the fear of God."—2 Cor. 7:1.

"For we are glad, when we are weak, and ye are strong: and this also we wish, even your perfection."

"Finally, brethren, farewell. Be perfect, be of good comfort, be of one mind, live in peace; and the God of love and peace shall be with you."—2 Cor. 13:9, 11.

"Therefore leaving the principles of the doctrine of Christ, let us go on to perfection; not laying again the foundation of repentance from dead works, and of faith toward God."—Heb. 6:1.

2. *Perfection is fully provided for.*

"It is God that girdeth me with strength, and maketh my way perfect."—Psa. 18:32.

"The Lord will perfect that which concerneth me."—Psa. 138:8.

"Since it is God himself who proposes to make us perfect, can there be any lack of power to accomplish the work? "As for God his way is perfect."—Psa. 18:30. "And the meek he will teach his way."—Psa. 25:9. Yea he "shall set us in the way of his steps."—Psa. 85:13. And "give his angels charge over us to keep us in his ways."—91:11. Therefore the righteous "do no iniquity: they walk in His ways."—119:3.

"And they shall sing in the ways of the Lord."
—138:5.

What a beautiful wreath of heavenly truth these Scriptures compose: and the same might be much enlarged. They show us that God's way is perfect, and he makes known to us his own precious way, and sets· our feet in the same, and keeps us therein. Praise his name! First, then, among the provisions for our perfection may be set down the infinite God Himself. All the power and wisdom of the Omnipotent are pledged to make us· perfect, and preserve us blameless. Who then can say we cannot be perfect in this life?

But this is not all. Speaking of "his saints," —*are you one of them?*—we read, "To whom God would make known what is the riches of the glory of this mystery among the Gentiles, which is Christ in you, the hope of glory: whom we preach, warning every man, and teaching every man in all wisdom, that we may *present every man perfect* in Christ Jesus."—Col. 1:27, 28. The revelation of Christ is given to make us perfect.

"Epaphras, who is one of you, a servant of Christ, saluteth you, always laboring fervently for you in prayers, that ye may stand perfect and complete in all the will of God."—Col. 4:12.

The ministry of Christ are commissioned to
make the saints perfect, and complete in all the
will of God. "And he gave some, apostles; and
some, prophets; and some, evangelists; and
some, pastors and teachers; for the perfecting
of the saints, for the work of the ministry, for
the edifying of the body of Christ:"—Eph. 4:11,
12. "All scripture is given by inspiration of God,
and is profitable for doctrine, for reproof, for
correction, for instruction in righteousness: That
the man of God may be perfect, thoroughly fur-
nished unto all good works."—2 Tim. 3:16, 17.
All scripture is given us of God for the purpose of
making every real man of God perfect. Are
you a man of God? If not, that accounts for the
fact you cannot believe in and receive this state
of Christian perfection.

"For the law made nothing perfect, but the
bringing in of a better hope did; by the which
we draw nigh unto God."—Heb. 7:19.

"For by one offering he hath perfected for
ever them that are sanctified."—Heb. 10:14.

"Now the God of peace, that brought again
from the dead our Lord Jesus, that great Shepherd of the sheep, through the blood of the
everlasting covenant, make you perfect in every
good work to do his will, working in you that

which is well pleasing in his sight, through Jesus Christ; to whom be glory for ever and ever. Amen.".—Heb. 13: 20, 21.   Surely we have provisions adequate to make us perfect.   All the fulness of the God-head.   The inspired Word, the living ministry, Jesus Christ himself, his perfect sacrifice, and precious blood, all vouchsafe to us this beautiful grace.   And is it still true that no one ever attained perfection?   We shall next prove that it has been attained both under the old and present dispensations.

3. Perfection has been attained.

"Nevertheless Asa's heart was perfect with the Lord all his days."—1 Kings 15:14.

"For the eyes of the Lord run to and fro throughout the whole earth, to show himself strong in the behalf of them whose heart is perfect toward him."—2 Chro. 16:9.   Would the all-wise God be looking about in all the earth to show his power in men whose hearts are perfect, if no such ever live in this world?

"There was a man in the land of Uz, whose name was Job; and that man was perfect and upright, and one that feared God, and eschewed evil."—Job 1:1.

"And the Lord said unto Satan, Hast thou considered my servant Job, that there is none like him in the earth, a perfect and an upright man, one that feareth God, and escheweth evil?" —Job 1:8. It appears from what follows the above that Satan was no believer in perfection of holy character. He ascribed Job's righteousness to selfish motives, as a means of earthly prosperity. He suggested that if God would put forth his hand and touch all he had Job would curse him to his face. But God, who knows what is in all men, had confidence in Job's holiness as being pure and unselfish. So he subjected the man whom he pronounces perfect to all the tests that Satan had asked for. He permitted the devil to take all his property, and with it his children and his health. Though great and unaccountable affliction and mental distress made him wish he never had been born, yet in all this great trial, "Job sinned not, nor charged God foolishly."—1:22. But he came out of the furnace as he went in, accepted of God. 42:8, 9. So God's testimony of Job's perfection proved good, and Satan's derogation a lie. Thank God for the book of Job! Among other precious things it clearly shows us that God is on the side of perfection, and Satan and his cursed unbelief stand against it. Reader, this fact will help you to determine whether you

are of God or of the devil. God's truth teaches
and his saints live out Christian perfection.
While Satan, even after proved a liar in Job's
case, and in thousands of others whom he has
questioned, is still base enough to keep up the
cry, "none perfect," "none perfect." And it is a
lamentable thing that he has in his employ even
many professed ministers of the gospel, all well
trained in Sinumust College.

Let us now hear the testimony of David:
"Mark the perfect man, and behold the upright;
for the end of that man is peace."—Psa. 37: 37.

"Who—the wicked—whet their tongues like
a sword, and bend their bows to shoot their
arrows, even bitter words: that they may shoot
in secret at the perfect."—Psa. 64: 3, 4.

"Mine eyes shall be upon the faithful of the
land, that they may dwell with me: he that
walketh in a perfect way, he shall serve me."
—Psa. 101: 6.

Why the command to "mark the perfect
man," if none be perfect? And how could the
wicked shoot at the perfect, if no such characters exist on earth? Again, how could God's
eyes be upon the perfect of the land, if there be
no perfect in the land?

Hear now the testimony of Hezekiah: "Remember now, O Lord, I beseech thee, how I have walked before thee in truth and with a perfect heart, and have done that which is good in thy sight."—Isa. 38: 3.

Dear reader, can you look God in the face, and with confidence make such an appeal? If you have walked before God in truth and with a perfect heart, you can testify to him in the same holy boldness.

The following texts abundantly prove the attainment of Christian perfection under the new covenant.

"Howbeit, we speak wisdom among them that are perfect."—1 Cor. 2: 6. "And ye are complete in him, which is the head of all principality and power."—Col. 2: 10. The word *pleroo*, here rendered "complete," means to be filled up, fully supplied, wanting nothing, etc., and is equivalent to perfection. Paul had the privilege of preaching to perfect men, hence there were such in his day.

"Let us, therefore, as many as be perfect, be thus minded."—Phil. 3: 15. In verses 11, 12, the apostle, speaking of the "resurrection of the dead," calls it a perfection which he had not yet attained. Many either willfully or ignorantly pervert his words into a denial of perfection in Christian grace, when all can see he speaks of the resurrection of the body, and final rewards. But these are careful to pass by in silence his words in verse 15, where he speaks of perfection already attained.

We have now proved that there is a state of grace called perfection, clearly commanded, fully provided for, and actually attained and witnessed to in this life. This leads to the inquiry, What is it? Doubtless many disbelieve in perfection because they associate it with something which is not provided for in this life. But while we accept the plain scriptural statements of present perfection in Christ, let us also qualify and apply the term as the scriptures do. We will here confine ourselves to the New Testament. The standard is raised by the Lord in Matt. 5: 48. "Perfect even as your Father which is in heaven is perfect." It is evident that the state consists in being like God in some particulars. Let the Word point out what they are.

1. "Pure even as he is pure."—1 Jno. 3: 3.

2. "Righteous even as he is."—Matt. 6: 33. 2 Cor. 5: 21. 1 Jno. 3: 7.

3. "Partaking his holiness."—2 Cor. 7: 1. Heb. 12: 10.

4. "Perfected love."—1 John 4: 17.

5. "Perfect patience."—Jas. 1: 4. Col. 1: 11.

6. "Perfect faith."—1 Thess. 3: 10. Heb. 12:2. Rom. 1: 17. 1 Cor. 13: 7.

Perfection of Christian character is then a present experience, and is the result of salvation. Hence it is not the result of any extraordinary birthright, nor is it through education, growth, or self culture. But "by one offering he—Christ—hath perfected forever them that are sanctified."—Heb. 10: 14. It is here declared identical with entire sanctification, and sanctification is salvation. "Because God hath from the beginning chosen you to salvation through sanctification of the Spirit, and belief of the truth."—2 Thess. 2: 13. We praise the Lord our God that the perfect Christ has provided us with a perfect salvation which makes us perfect Christians, and preserves us "holy and unblameable and unreproveable in his sight."

———▶•◀———

8th. SALVATION FITS US FOR HEAVEN.

What is the fitness needed to enter and enjoy that holy place of God's awful presence? If we

will attend to the voice of inspiration no man
need be deceived in this matter.

"Blessed are the pure in heart, for they shall
see God."—Matt. 5: 8. "Follow peace with all
men, and holiness, without which no man shall
see the Lord."—Heb. 12: 14.

Reader, do you now perceive why God created
man in his own image? He designed that his
intelligent creatures should enjoy the fellowship
and companionship of their Creator. But this
can only take place on the plane of his nature,
in the possession of his own holiness. Hence,
also, the injunction, "Be ye holy, for I am holy."
—1 Pet. 1: 16. According to the very nature of
the case, no person in this world, or in the
world to come, can enjoy, or even endure the
divine presence and glory unless transformed
into the same image, and filled with his glory.
Daniel was a righteous man, and yet he was
"afraid and fell upon his face" (Dan. 8: 17), at
the approach of Gabriel, an angel from God's
presence. The Apostle John was a wholly
sanctified man of God, and yet when he saw the
Almighty Redeemer whose "countenance was
as the sun shineth in his strength, fell at his feet
as dead."—Rev. 1: 16, 17. Though morally fitted
to enjoy God, the resurrection and glorification

of the body was yet wanting. How, then, can any soul with the smallest spot of sin hope to stand before God in the awful day of his coming and judgment? "Wherefore, beloved, seeing that ye look for such things, be diligent that ye may be found of him in peace, without spot, and blameless."—2 Pet. 3: 14. O how many plain and solemn warnings God has given all men of that day when all must stand or fall in the presence of his majesty and glory, when the earth and the works thereof shall be burned up! "Seeing then that all these things shall be dissolved, what manner of persons ought ye to be in all holy conversation and godliness?"—2 Pet. 3: 11.

Reader, are you a candidate for heaven and eternal glory? Then mark well the conditions upon which you must take your crown, and in the default of which you must sink to an awful doom. How think you the gates of heaven will be guarded against the entrance of unworthy characters? We read of no mighty angel, who, with all-penetrating eyes shall examine those who would enter there. How then will the purity of heaven be protected? Find an answer in 2 Thess. 1: 7–9.

"And to you who are troubled rest with us, when the Lord Jesus shall be revealed from heaven with his mighty angels, **in** flaming fire taking vengeance on them that know not God, and that obey not the gospel of our Lord Jesus Christ: who shall be punished with everlasting destruction from the presence of the Lord, and from the glory of his power."

At the same time we are **told** he will "be glorified in his saints, and admired in all them that believe." So let it be known once for all that all who are unfit for heaven will be driven back to hell "from the presence of the Lord, and from the glory of his power." Though heaven's gates stand wide open before all men, no person will enter with a stain of sin upon his soul. No unholy man can endure the presence of God and his divine glory. The hottest place in hell were a relief to the soul unsaved and out of Christ.

A wit once said in a New York paper that he dreamed a certain man, prominent in his circle, had died, and approached the gates of heaven, where he was told, "YOU MAY COME IN BUT YOU WILL NOT LIKE IT." A mighty truth was unwittingly uttered by the thoughtless sinner. Oh that the Almighty may make men to consider that heaven were worse than hell itself for all who are not of heavenly temper! Oh how sad and sickening the sight of our present evil world, and its awful destiny so near! The masses who profess the Christian name, know they are sinful and unholy, and yet hope to stop sinning when safe in heaven. We used to hear them sing with much animation,

"If I only get to heaven, If I only get to heaven,
　If I only get to heaven when I die."

They hope to see the beautiful gate ajar for them, and if they may only be permitted to slip into the golden city, imagine they will be all right. Oh how awful will be their disappointment! The very holiness of heaven will drive them back in terror. Jesus knew very well that men would base their eternal happiness on merely getting into heaven, and has given us a parable to show all men how such a faith will terminate. He tells of one who came in without the "wedding garment;" but he did not enjoy it. He was speechless, and was bound hand and foot, and cast out into outer darkness; "there shall be weeping and gnashing of teeth."— Matt. 22: 11–13. Nothing but the spotless robe of perfect holiness will make heaven a heaven for you.

"Be not deceived, God is not mocked." None but the pure in heart can enter there and see

God in peace. Yea, in the light of God's truth
we cry aloud and say unto all, you must be as
pure as heaven to enter and enjoy that holy
place. And, thanks be to the God of all grace
and mercy, SALVATION will put you in that condition and preserve you ready to enter and enjoy
all the glory of heaven. Many scriptures prove
the fact. "For by one offering, he, Christ, hath
perfected forever them that are sanctified."—
Heb. 10: 14. This does not mean that the holy
state cannot be forfeited; but that entire sanctification perfects our salvation from sin, and puts
us on the plane of heaven's purity. Hence, if
that grace is retained no further cleansing is
needed forever. Therefore, Christ "being made
perfect—a perfect Savior—became the author
of eternal salvation unto all them that obey
him." The law was a temporary system; it made
nothing perfect; but the bringing in of a better
hope—Christ—did. In him we have come to
the final and complete redemption, that fits us
for the society of God through all remaining
time and eternity.

"And the very God of peace sanctify you
wholly; and I pray God your whole spirit and
soul and body be preserved blameless unto the
coming of our Lord Jesus Christ. Faithful is

he that calleth you, who also will do it."—
1 Thess. 5: 23, 24.

"And you, that were sometime alienated and
enemies in your mind by wicked works, yet now
hath he reconciled in the body of his flesh
through death, to present you holy and unblameable and unreproveable in his sight."—
Col. 1: 21, 22.

"Who are kept by the power of God through
faith unto salvation ready to be revealed in the
last time."—1 Pet. 1: 5.

"Herein is our love made perfect, that we
may have boldness in the day of judgment: because as he is, so are we in this world."—1
John 4: 17.

These scriptures clearly and positively affirm
that the salvation of God sanctifies us soul, body,
and spirit, and preserves us blameless. "Kept
by the power of God through faith unto salvation, ready to be revealed in the last day."
Even as Christ is, so are we in this world, and
therefore will have boldness in the day of
judgment.

There is, therefore, no purgatory needed by
the Christian. Nor is such a thing taught in
the scripture. Nor yet that other deception of
Satan; namely, extreme unction. SALVATION is

God's extreme unction; the fulness of his power revealed in us; keeping us blameless and spotless in his sight. And, "So an entrance shall be ministered unto you abundantly, into the everlasting kingdom of our Lord and Savior Jesus Christ."—2 Pet. I: II.

9th. IT IS GOD'S SALVATION.

Salvation is a plan, a remedy, which has for its object the restoration of man from the power of sin and the effects of the fall. Now any project should command attention and confidence in proportion to the greatness of its author. Who has conceived and devised the plan of salvation? Thus it is written: "Salvation belongeth unto the Lord." He is the sole originator and proprietor of this most stupendous undertaking and marvelous business that has ever been opened upon earth. Therefore, "The *salvation* of the righteous is of the LORD."—Psa. 37: 39. And thus hath Jehovah spoken to his anointed: "I will also give thee for a light unto the Gentiles, that thou mayest be MY SALVATION unto the ends of the earth."—Isa. 49: 6. Here we learn that the Son of God is the only authorized mediator and embodiment of *God's salvation*. To him, therefore, every human being must either apply and be saved; or, if refusing or neglecting to do so, in the day of judgment stand condemned "of sin because they believed not on him."—John 16: 9. "Because they believed not in God, and trusted not in *his salvation*."—Psa. 78: 22. When, therefore, good old Simeon saw the infant Redeemer, he embraced him, saying, "Lord, now lettest thou thy servant depart in peace, according to thy word; for mine eyes have seen *thy salvation*."—Luke 2: 29, 30. Salvation belongeth unto God, and Jesus Christ is his salvation. Bless his dear name! No person can ignore the Son and be saved by the Father, nor despise the Father without rejecting the Son. Luke 10: 6. Let it be distinctly understood that God has so arranged the plan of redemption that no man or set of men can monopolize, control, or get a patent upon it. God has offered a FREE SALVATION to all the world, and it is impossible for the most crafty to convert it into a means of speculation. It is true there are money-run religions many, and hirelings many. But "the hireling is not the shepherd;" not sent of God: and the money-making religions are frauds.

Salvation is "without money and without price;" therefore, whoever would set a price upon it, proves he is not in possession of the article himself, and has but a counterfeit to offer. Every man on earth can come directly to the Author of salvation through Jesus Christ, and be saved independent of all men or angels.

Dear reader, be sure that you get the genuine article, the salvation that really saves. Remember there is only one firm in control of the business. Only one name under heaven whereby ye must be saved. All modern organizations are frauds. Though they offer you cheap terms, a broad road, and a flesh-pleasing policy, there is death in the end. Be sure and get your salvation direct from God through his Son. See that your ticket for heaven has upon it the seal of the living God. If you have religion and yet a sinner, you have been badly taken in. You have dealt with the wrong firm. For your soul's sake cast away your religion, and seek God's salvation. Thus call upon him: "O visit me with *thy salvation!*"—Psa. 106:4. "Show us thy mercy, O Lord, and grant us *thy salvation.*"—Psa. 85: 7.

Stop your ears to every other offer, and be satisfied with nothing short of God's true and only salvation.

If you have a religion which has not "raised you up together, and made you sit together in heavenly places in Christ Jesus" (Eph. 2:6), you have not found God's salvation, and you are yet on too low a plane to enter heaven. You should come to him with this earnest prayer, "Let *thy salvation*, O God, set me up on high."— Psa. 69: 29.

If you have not had a salvation that lasts all the year round with uninterrupted peace and victory in your soul, God says to you, *"My salvation shall be forever."*—Isa. 51: 6.

If the darts of the wicked one and the powers of hell oppress and overcome your soul, for Christ's sake do not think you must remain in that wretched condition. Acquaint yourself with God, and get an experience where you can joyfully say to him, "Thou hast also given me the *shield of thy salvation*, and thy right hand hath holden me up, and thy gentleness hath made me great."—Psa. 18: 35.

If your heart is not joyful, but gloomy, you have not been blessed with the salvation of the Lord. Seek him with all your heart; then shall ye break forth in praise to God, saying, "Lo, this is our God; we have waited for him and he will save us; this is the LORD; we have waited for him; we will be glad, and rejoice in *his salvation.*"—Isa. 25: 9. Yea, "In *thy salvation* how greatly shall we rejoice?"—Psa. 21: 1. Thank God for his perfect salvation! Reader, are you really in possession of it?

———▶•◀———

10th. GOD HIMSELF IS OUR SALVATION.

The holy prophet Isaiah seemed to have been filled with surprise and admiration at the revelation of this wonderful truth to his mind. Hence he cries out, "Behold, *God is my salvation;* I will trust, and not be afraid: for the LORD JEHOVAH is my strength and my song; he also is become my *salvation.* Therefore with joy shall ye draw water out of the wells of salvation."—Isa. 12: 2, 3.

Surely we should draw water in abundance and with great joy from a well so deep, so boundless, and so glorious.

When the children of Israel stood upon the wilderness side of the Red sea, and beheld the waters of God's judgment swallowing up their enemies, they sang this song: "The Lord is my strength and song, and he is become *my salvation.*"—Ex. 15: 2.

When David was beset by many and great foes, and his life was chased and hunted like a wild roe, he turned to God with this prayer: "Say unto my soul, I am *thy salvation.*"—Psa. 35: 3. But we need not now ask God to speak this word to our soul. He has clearly declared himself, and freely offers himself to be the perfect salvation of all those who put their trust in him.

"He only is my rock and my salvation."— Psa. 62: 2. "The Lord is my strength and song; and is become my salvation."—Psa. 118: 14.

"The Lord is my light and my salvation, whom shall I fear? The Lord is the strength of my life; of whom shall I be afraid?"–Psa. 27: 1.

What precious and soul-cheering truth! With God, the Almighty, for our salvation, and he the strength of our life, well may it be asked, What shall we fear?

"Truly in the Lord our God is the salvation of Israel."—Jer. 3: 23.

Many other scriptures identify our salvation with God. What a wonderful announcement to lost and helpless humanity! Surely no person can read and believe these scriptures and yet think of salvation as something limited, and insufficient to meet the utmost wants of fallen man. If the Almighty is our salvation, then it can do for us all that lies in the power of God to do. And there is nothing too hard for him. Is God able to create worlds? to call forth into being that which had no being? Behold, all things were made by him. Then if man was so utterly destroyed by the fall that nothing short of a new creation could save him, thank God the power is at hand to meet the demand. And such is actually the work of our redemption. "Therefore, if any man be in Christ there is a *new creation:* old things are passed away; behold, all things are become new; and all things are of God."—2 Cor. 5: 17, 18. "For in Christ Jesus neither circumcision availeth anything, nor uncircumcision, but a *new creation.*" —Gal. 6: 15. We quote the rendering of Rotherham, Emphatic Diaglott, and many other translations. A new creation takes place in our restoration from the death and ruin of sin. God only possesses creative power. So he is become our salvation. No wonder we read of a "great salvation." It is as great as God himself. My soul doth make its boast in the Lord, and stand triumphant over all the powers of sin, of earth and hell; having for its salvation the greatest and most mighty One of the whole universe.

Therefore, in many respects at least, what may be affirmed of God is also true of our salvation. If God is holy so is our salvation; and it invests us with the same moral quality.

"God is love." So is our salvation. Only he whose very life and being is love is in possession of salvation. The two elements are inseparable. Therefore we read that "the gift of prophecy," "all knowledge," "all faith," benevolence that gives all our goods to feed the poor; and a zeal that delivers our body to be burned at the stake, will profit us nothing without love. The salvation of all men is guaged by the measure of the pure love of God shed abroad in the heart by the Holy Spirit, and manifest in our life.—1 Cor. 13: 1–3.

Is God almighty? So is our salvation. The energy of omnipotence is the arm of our deliverance.

"O God the Lord, the *strength of my salvation*, thou hast covered my head in the day of battle."—Psa. 140: 7.

"The God of my rock; in him will I trust: he is my shield, and the horn of my salvation, my high tower, and my refuge, my Savior."—2 Sam. 22: 3.

"The Lord is my rock, and my fortress, and

my deliverer; my God, my strength, in whom I will trust; my buckler, and the horn of my salvation, and my high tower."—Psa. 18: 2.

How can Satan and all his hosts stand before us, or prevail over us, having a salvation that has God for its strength? He is the horn of our salvation. Anciently horns were worn upon the cap to denote office, rank and authority. So our salvation ranks with the power and authority of Jehovah. O praise God for such a salvation!

God is eternal. So is our salvation. "And being made perfect, he became the author of eternal salvation unto all them that obey him." —Heb. 5: 9.

God has become our salvation, by his divine incarnation in the person of his Son, in whose body a complete sacrifice was made for our sins. He has become our salvation because his love reaches even to us, in the low depths of our wretchedness. He has become our salvation by clothing our souls in his own beautiful righteousness, wherein we can stand in his presence without fear, with great joy. Again he has become our salvation by infusing his own holy life in us, which enables us to walk in the steps of him who did no sin. Finally, he has become our salvation by giving us the sure covenant of his mercy, in which all his honor and integrity is pledged to save to the uttermost all that come to him through Jesus Christ. O beloved, if you would but properly consider this one fact, all your groveling ideas of our possibilities in divine grace would vanish away. Think of it; the great Jehovah has bound himself in an everlasting covenant, sealed by the blood of his own Son, and has even sworn to by himself, that he would fully save every soul that believes on him. He has thus obligated himself, and all the immutability and veracity of his holy character back up his words of eternal life. Oh what assurance his promises must inspire when we think that they are as firm as God himself! While I stand upon his Word, and obey his precious will, he has made himself responsible for my constant salvation. And "he has magnified his Word above all his name." Bless his holy name forever!

------◆◆◆------

11th. SALVATION LEAVES NO CLOAK FOR SIN.

By nearly all sin-serving professors it is admitted that the Bible requires us to be pure and holy, and to live free from sin. But most of them claim that we cannot in this life meet those requirements. That the commands, "be ye holy," "be ye perfect," etc., are simply set before us as the standard toward which we should ever approach, but cannot, while living in this world, hope to attain. For instance, before us is a letter from a man who subscribes his name, *Stixtus*, from Brookville, Pa., in which the sectish Dunkard seeks to cloak over his sins. He speaks against what he calls our "ridiculous attempt to bolster up that old and long since exploded doctrine of perfect sanctification in this life." On the next page appear hese words: "All admit that perfect sanctification ought to be, and in fact is the aim of every child of God in every stage of his progress here on earth. *It is also certainly true that God requires all capable and responsible men everywhere to be holy as he is holy, and perfect as he is perfect.* No one denies this, or in fact ever did deny it. The real question is simply this: Are true believers all they ought to be? Are they as holy, as perfect, as sinless, as they ought to be, and as God requires them to be? The true church universal answers emphatically in the negative. The reply of your dupes is an emphatic yes.

Thus you, in effect, say, we are as holy, as perfect, as sinless, and immaculate as we ought to be, or in fact can be. From this it follows that those who claim to be perfectly sanctified in this life will not be, and do not expect to be any more holy, sinless, or spotless, when singing the song of redeeming love in heaven, than they are here on earth.

"The apostle says, speaking of true believers after death, 'We shall be like him [Christ], for we shall see him as he is.' But those who believe in perfect sanctification in this life, as represented by you, believe themselves now to be as pure, as holy, and as sinless, as the Lord Jesus Christ. Permit me to say that such a belief is simply disgusting to any one who realizes that the human heart is deceitful above all things, and desperately wicked. It is worse than disgusting; it is blasphemy."

"Let us notice some of the leading passages of scripture you rely on to give authority to your belief. 'Be ye holy for I am holy.' 'Be ye perfect even as your Father in heaven is perfect.' These commandments you seem to think prove that the true believer is holy in this life. This simply proves your lamentable ignorance of the scriptures. These commandments declare what the true believer *ought to be* and *must be*, not what he really is, your arrogant gabble to the contrary notwithstanding."

How does this last sentence sound from a man who accuses us with being "scurrilous to the extreme in most, if not all, our articles?" Nay, Mr. Stixtus, we have no time nor inclination to condescend to such words. "For the weapons of our warfare are not carnal, but mighty through God." We have no need of anything stronger than the truth, nor sharper than the word of God.

This disputer of the power of God to fulfill in us his Word, and make us what we ought to be, is a fair sample of Babylon confusion in general. He calls the doctrine of "perfect sanctification in this life," "old and long since exploded." And yet admits that it is just what God requires of all men everywhere. So the man seems to think that the requirement of God is long since exploded, *i. e.*, proved a fallacy. But, says he, "The real question is simply this: Are true believers all they ought to be? Are they as holy, as perfect, as sinless as they ought to be, as God requires them to be?" That is always the way with hirelings. "The real question" with them is not what God requires, and what men "ought

to be;" but what they are, and what will please
them. He would have us drop the standard of
the divine requirement, because the masses of
sectism are far below it. How forcibly the
words of the apostle apply here. "For do I
now persuade men, or God? or do I seek to
please men? for if I yet pleased men, I should
not be the servant of Christ."—Gal. 1: 10.
There is a variance between God and the people.
He requires them to be holy, perfect and spotless in his sight. But they are far from this.
So if they become one with God, he will have to
come to them, or they to him. He must either
recall his commandments, or the people measure to them. What shall we, as God's embas-
sadors, do in the case? "Do we persuade men
or God?" Persuade him to modify his Word, or
the people to change their ways? "Or do I
seek to please men?" God forbid; "for if I yet
pleased men, I should not be the servant of
Christ."

This man-pleasing and God-dishonoring policy is all foretold in prophecy. "Which say to
the seers, see not, and to the prophets, prophesy
not unto us right things; speak unto us smooth
things; prophesy deceits."—Isa. 30: 10.

"Shall I not visit for these things? saith the

Lord: shall not my soul be avenged on such a nation as this? A wonderful and horrible thing is committed in the land; the prophets prophesy falsely, and the priests bear rule by their means; and my people love to have it so: and what will ye do in the end thereof?"—Jer. 5:29-31.

The position taken by crooked *Stixtus* is virtually this: "God requires all capable and responsible men everywhere to be holy as he is holy," etc. But all men everywhere—down in Babylon where he lives—are unholy and imperfect. Therefore, what God requires is "old and exploded." Well, if we accept the standard of Babylon, God's word is exploded and fallen; but, on the other hand, if we accept the Bible standard, behold, Babylon is exploded and fallen. Which is true? "A voice from heaven" answers, "Babylon the great is fallen, is fallen, and is become the habitation of devils, and the hold of every foul spirit."—Rev. 18: 2.

But we might apply the above logic with equal propriety to repentance and a hundred other demands of God that the people come short of. It is certainly true that God requires all capable and responsible men everywhere to repent of their sins. But the real question is simply this: Have the world of sinners and

5

professors repented as they should? By no means. Therefore the doctrine of genuine repentance in this life is an "old and long since exploded" thing. And all who teach it are "lamentably ignorant," and all who believe their teaching, "dupes." The reasoning is the same; and if it has any weight against perfect sanctification, it weighs equally against repentance and justification. But of course it is ridiculous falsehood, blind confusion.

According to this strange Stixtus, a *"true believer"* is one that does not believe the truth, is "not what he ought to be, nor what God requires him to be." But a man that really believes the word of God, and lives and testifies accordingly is pronounced "lamentably ignorant," "disgusting," "blasphemer."

"Woe unto them that call evil good, and good evil; that put darkness for light, and light for darkness; that put bitter for sweet, and sweet for bitter! Woe unto them that are wise in their own eyes, and prudent in their own sight!" —Isa. 5: 20, 21.

After quoting, "Be ye holy for I am holy," "Be ye perfect even as your Father which is in heaven is perfect," "Darkness-for-light" says: "These commandments you seem to think prove that the true believer is holy in this life. This simply proves your lamentable ignorance of the scriptures. These commandments declare *what the true believer ought to be and must be*, not what he really is."

We confess that we are very ignorant indeed of all scriptures which teach that a true believer is yet an unholy man. That he is not what he *"ought to be,"* nor what he *"must be."* Our knowledge of the Bible is so limited that we have not learned how a man can serve two masters; can be a Christian and a sinner at the same time. We have never yet learned in that sacred volume that a "good tree can bring forth evil fruit, nor an evil tree good fruit." Nor have we attained that modern wisdom which maintains that a *true believer* is one who does not believe the word of God, and he that does believe and teach the same is a blasphemer.

Our friend Stixtus is greatly shocked by the testimony of God's children that the blood of Christ has made us "as holy, as perfect, as sinless as we ought to be." Will he please prove by the Word that it is consistent, and to the glory of God to be anything else? Remember that all we contend for in the provisions of divine grace he admits we ought to be, and must be, and God requires it of us. There is no question of this. But the real question with him is, "Are we all we ought to be?" A very questionable thing in Babylon. But this has nothing to do with the word of God, nor yet with those who have come out of her and are *"complete in Him* who is the head of all principality and power." God pity the dwellers in the dark city of confusion. Like the disciples of Christ who became offended at the words of Christ. The very thing they admit God requires of all his children they pronounce a "hard saying." "Thus you in effect say, we are as holy, as perfect, as sinless, as we ought to be, or in fact can be," and "do not expect to be any more holy, sinless, or spotless, when singing the song of redeeming love in heaven than you are here on earth." To all of which we answer, Why not? Read the preceding chapters, and answer before the Almighty, Where is there a cloak to cover your sins? What man is fool enough to think he can stand before the judgment bar of God and say, "Lord, we knew you required all capable and responsible men everywhere to be holy as you are holy, and perfect as you are perfect. No one denies this, but we confess we are not as holy, as perfect, as sinless

as we ought to be, and as God requires us to be.
But this is our plea: We could not be what you
demanded of us." Will you thus stand before
the bar of God and make him a liar who says,
"My grace is sufficient for thee?" And in a
thousand other promises which leave absolutely
nothing wanting to perfect in holiness and preserve blameless in soul and body, in heart and
life, all who are willing and obedient? Will you
say to the Judge, "Our preachers told us we
could not be pure and perfect while living in
the flesh?" Then shall the Judge say, "I never
sent them."—Jer. 23: 21, 22. "For he whom God
hath sent speaketh the words of God."—John
3: 34. "Cursed be the man that trusteth in man,
and maketh flesh his arm, and whose heart
departeth from the Lord."—Jer. 17: 5.

Again we ask, Why not be pure and holy and
sinless in this life? Was not Christ "manifest
to take away our sin, and in him is no sin?" Is
it not true that the blood of Jesus Christ cleanseth us from all sin? Are we not "kept by the
power of God through faith unto salvation,
ready to be revealed in the last time?" Is not
the power of God sufficient to do all this for us?

Thus answers Stixtus: "The apostle says,
speaking of true believers after death, 'We shall

be like him [Christ], for we shall see him as he is.'" This is a perversion of the word of God, a quiet, soothing deception of the devil. The reference is to 1 John 3: 2, 3.

"Beloved, now are we the sons of God, and it doth not yet appear what we shall be: but we know that, when he shall appear, we shall be like him; for we shall see him as he is. And every man that hath this hope in him purifieth himself, even as he is pure."—1 Jno. 3: 2, 3.

While this includes saints of God whose bodies have fallen asleep, it does not refer to a condition that was produced by death, nor is it confined to the departed; but equally refers to the faithful who will be living at the instant of Christ's coming. "We shall see him as he is," in the morning of his glorious coming, and shall be found like him. We know there will a change take place then which will fashion our mortal bodies like unto his glorious body. That will be the resurrection. But that change is not alluded to in the above words. Else would the apostle have said, "When he comes we shall be made like him." But he refers to the moral condition into which the grace of God has transformed us. The "image" of our Creator (Col. 3: 10), which is perfect holiness. This is positively proved in the next verse. "We shall be like him; for we shall see him as he is. And every man that hath this hope in him *purifieth himself even as he* [Christ], *is pure.*"—1 Jno. 3: 2, 3. Whoever expects to be like Christ, must attain that condition before his coming; must purify himself even as Christ is pure. Then, of course, he will be like him when he appears. The third verse explains the second. To be like Christ is to be sanctified wholly, "pure in heart;" for such the Savior said shall see him. The same state is again referred to in chapter 4, verse 17. "Herein is our love made perfect, that we may have boldness in the day of judgment; because as he is so are we in this world."

This does not defer the likeness of Christ in our soul until the next world. It does not speak of a state after death. But our love being made perfect we are already like him. This state is not produced by death, but love made perfect is the result of heart purity. A heart so perfectly cleansed by the blood of Christ, that nothing remains but the love of God, shed abroad by the Holy Spirit. Perfect purity and perfect love are co-relative, and inclusive of each other.

So the only text cited to prove that we will

not be like Christ until after death, with its context proves that we are like him in this life. "*As he is so are we in this world.*" Reader, are you now, in this world, like Christ in moral purity, as he sits at the right hand of the throne of God? If not, your hope to stand in the day of judgment will prove a fatal delusion.

Observe that the opposer of Bible sanctification in this life, freely admits that we ought to be holy and sinless in this life. Even said we "must be." Now these terms very positively enjoin moral obligation. If we ought to be holy, we are morally bound to be such. No doubt in other things he has told people that they could not enter heaven if they leave undone commands of Christ they ought to do. How, then, can he expect to stand in the day of judgment, if not what he ought to be in perfect holiness, and what God requires him to be? If a person can set aside God's law and solemn command, "Be ye holy," what part of the Bible is binding? Be not deceived, the word of God is forever settled in heaven, and will judge us in the last day. Then "*be ye holy*" will speak in thunder tones to all the unholy; will strike terror to their souls, and drive them back from the presence of God and the glory of his power. If not pure as

Christ in this life, some sin remains in you. Death will not remove sin. Therefore if you die in that condition, the judgment day will find you the same, and drive you from the presence of God.

But here is the key to Mr. Stixtus' unbelief: "Permit me to say that such a belief, *i. e.*, that of being pure, holy and sinless as Christ in this life,—such a belief is simply disgusting to any one who realizes that the human heart is deceitful above all things, and desperately wicked." Alas! here it all comes out what kind of a heart is back of this wretched unbelief in perfect sanctification. "Unto the pure all things are pure, but unto them that are defiled and unbelieving, is nothing pure; but even their mind and conscience is defiled."—Titus 1: 15. No wonder the man is so extremely disgusted with the idea of heart purity in this life; for "it is abomination to fools to depart from evil."—Prov. 13: 19.

Now we do not call in question the statement of the prophet that "the human heart is deceitful above all things and desperately wicked." But who is so blind as not to see that this refers to the human heart in its natural depraved state? Surely Jesus had reference to a very different

heart in the beatitude, "Blessed are the pure in
heart; for they shall see God." The application
of the description given by Jeremiah to Christians, and all indiscriminately, sadly betrays
ignorance of the work of heart cleansing in the
blood of Christ. Yea, his words clearly imply
that such is his own heart. Surely great darkness reigns in Babylon, else her teachers would
know better than to use the deceitful and
wicked hearts of sinners as a standard for
Christians, and hope thereby to cloak over their
sins. Surely if Hezekiah had been in possession
of a heart that was "desperately wicked," he
could not have testified in the face of God that
he had "walked before him in truth, and with a
perfect heart." If such were the case of Christian
hearts, we would like to know what Christ has
done for us? What virtue is there in his blood?
What benefit in his salvation? Then what did
Paul mean when he wrote Timothy to "follow
righteousness, faith, charity, peace, with them
that call on the Lord out of a *pure heart.*—2
Tim. 2: 22. Oh when will men cease to drag
the word of God and their obligations down on
a level with their deceitful hearts and unholy
lives, rather than measure their responsibilities
by the word of God, and then appropriate his

almighty grace to lift them up to its holy standard? One minute's reflection with common
sense upon the theme must lead every candid
mind to the conclusion that, since *salvation is of
God*, and is no more limited than the Infinite
himself, no person needs to fall short of what
he ought to be, what he must be, and what God
requires him to be. Who dare for a moment
deny that the Almighty is able to remove all
sin out of our entire being, restore our soul to
the same holy image in which he created man;
"bruise Satan under our feet," and give us power
over all the power of the adversary; "make a
way of escape in every temptation," and preserve us "holy and unblameable and unreproveable" in his sight; living free from sin every
moment and second of our lives? The omnipotence and omnipresence of God stop every
mouth! "Where is the disputer of this world"
that will question His ability to do these things
for us?

Then one of two things must inevitably follow. Either we can "live holy, and righteous,
and godly in this present world," or else God
can, but will not, keep us. If he will not do so,
then it is evident he does not want us to live
pure and holy; in other words he allows sin in

us, and justifies us in sin. Which would prove
that he himself has pleasure in unrighteousness.
And that would prove him unholy.

Again, let it be remembered that to make
and keep us perfect, pure and spotless, is just
what he has pledged himself to do in all his
"exceeding great and precious promises." If
he will not do so, his word fails, and his character is divested of truthfulness; which would
again strip him of holiness.

Then it follows that to doubt God's ability to
make and keep us perfect in holiness, denies his
infinity. And to question his willingness, is to
deny his holiness. Therefore, any attempt to
apologize for sin in any form and to any extent,
robs God of his attributes, and reduces him to
no God. Here then is the conclusion of the
whole matter: *The Christian is no sinner, or God is
no God.* Therefore, thus saith the Lord, "If I
had not come and spoken unto them, they had
not had sin: *but now they have no cloak for their
sins.*"—Jno. 15: 22. In the margin it is "*No excuse for sin.*" If, therefore, any man on earth
who has heard the gospel of God, supposes he
has an excuse for sin and uncleanness, for not
being what he "ought to be, and must be, and
what God requires him to be," he is deceived of

the adversary of his soul; and will hear at the bar of God, these awful words: "Depart from me, ye that work iniquity, for I never acknowledged you." Oh what multiplied thousands Satan has in this very trap! The words of Jesus are truly being fulfilled: "Many false prophets shall arise and shall deceive many." They, "having a form of godliness, but denying the power thereof: from such turn away."—2 Tim. 3: 5. Reader, for your soul's sake, *get saved in Jesus* from all sin, and live holy and unblameable before God. For if you are not what you ought to be now, you will be weighed in the balance and found wanting in the day of judgment.

———— • ————

12th. THE PROMISES OF SALVATION ARE AS GREAT AS THE COMMANDMENTS OF GOD.

———

As we have already observed, it is generally admitted that God s word demands of all men to live holy and sinless lives. But foolish men look at these high commands of God, then at their inward proneness to evil and impotency in that which is good; and also look at the world of wicked forces around them, and they say, "No man can keep the commands of the Lord."

But, dear reader, this is altogether unwise. Let us now look at the strongest commands of the Bible, and then place along side of them the corresponding promises of God. And we will see that no command exceeds the proffered grace of God to fulfill it in us. Let us weigh the two in opposite ends of the scales. Read one point at a time in both columns. We will begin with

HEART PURITY.

Commands.

"Wash you, make you clean; put away the evil of your doings from before mine eyes; cease to do evil."—Isa. 1: 16.

"Cleanse your hands, ye sinners; and purify your hearts, ye doubleminded."—Jas. 4: 8.

"Having therefore these promises, dearly beloved, let us cleanse ourselves from all filthiness of the flesh and spirit, perfecting holiness in the fear of God."—2 Cor. 7: 1.

Promises.

"Then will I sprinkle clean water upon you, and ye shall be clean: from all your filthiness, and from all your idols, will I cleanse you."—Eze. 36: 25.

"When the Lord shall have washed away the filth of the daughters of Zion, and shall have purged the blood of Jerusalem from the midst thereof by the spirit of judgment, and by the spirit of burning."—Isa. 4: 4.

"And the voice spake unto him again the second time, What God hath cleansed, that call not thou common."–Acts 10: 15.

A NEW HEART.

Commands.	*Promises.*
"Cast away from you all your transgressions, whereby ye have transgressed; and make you a new heart and a new spirit: for why will ye die, O house of Israel?"—Eze. 18: 31.	"A new heart also will I give you, and a new spirit will I put within you: and I will take away the stony heart out of your flesh, and I will give you a heart of flesh."—Eze. 36: 26.

BE RIGHTEOUS AS CHRIST IS RIGHTEOUS.

Commands.	*Promises.*
"Thy people also shall be all righteous: they shall inherit the land forever, the branch of my planting, the work of my hands, that I may be glorified." —Isa. 60: 21.	"For he hath made him to be sin for us, who knew no sin; that we might be made the righteousness of God in him."—2 Cor. 5: 21.
"Little children, let no man deceive you: he that doeth righteousness is righteous, even as he is righteous."—1 Jno. 3: 7.	"For the grace of God that bringeth salvation hath appeared to all men, teaching us that, denying ungodliness and worldly lusts, we should live soberly, righteously, and godly, in this present world."—Tit. 2: 11, 12.

BE YE HOLY.

Commands.	*Promises.*
"But as he which hath called you is holy, so be ye holy in all manner of conversation; because it is written, Be ye holy; for I am holy."—1 Pet. 1: 15,16.	"Having therefore, brethren, boldness to enter into the holiest by the blood of Jesus."-Heb. 10:19.
According as he hath chosen us in him before the foundation of the world, that we should be	"For they verily for a few days chastened us after their own pleasure; but he for our profit, that

holy and without blame before him in love."—Eph. 1: 4.

"Follow peace with all men, and holiness, without which no man shall see the Lord."—Heb.12:14.

we might be partakers of his holiness."—Heb.12:10.

"For if the firstfruit be holy, the lump is also holy: and if the root be holy, so are the branches."—Rom. 11: 16.

ENTIRE SANCTIFICATION.

Commands.

"But sanctify the Lord God in your hearts: and be ready always to give an answer to every man that asketh you a reason of the hope that is in you, with meekness and fear."—1 Pet. 3: 15.

"For this is the will of God, even your sanctification, that ye should abstain from fornication."—1 Thess. 4: 3.

"But we are bound to give thanks always to God for you, brethren beloved of the Lord, because God hath from the beginning chosen you to salvation through sanctification of the Spirit and belief of the truth."—2 Thess. 2: 13.

Promises.

"And for their sakes I sanctify myself, that they also might be sanctified through the truth."—John 17: 19.

"Wherefore Jesus also, that he might sanctify the people with his own blood, suffered without the gate."—Heb. 13: 12.

"And the very God of peace sanctify you wholly; and I pray God your whole spirit and soul and body be preserved blameless unto the coming of our Lord Jesus Christ. Faithful is he that calleth you, who also will do it."—1 Thess. 5: 23, 24.

"That I should be the minister of Jesus Christ to the Gentiles, ministering the gospel of God, that the offering up of the Gentiles might be acceptable, being sanctified by the Holy Ghost."—Rom. 15: 16.

BE YE PERFECT.

Commands.

"Thou shalt be perfect with the Lord thy God."—Deut. 18: 13.

"Be ye, therefore, perfect, even as your Father which is in heaven is perfect."—Matt. 5: 48.

Promises.

"It is God that girdeth me with strength and maketh my way perfect."—Psa. 18: 32.

"Now the God of peace, that brought again from the dead our Lord Jesus, that great Shepherd of the sheep, through the blood of the everlasting covenant, make you perfect in every good work to do his will, working in you that which is well pleasing in his sight, through Jesus Christ; to whom be glory forever and ever. Amen."—Heb. 13: 20, 21.

LOVE GOD WITH ALL THY HEART.

Command.

"And thou shalt love the Lord thy God with all thine heart, and with all thy soul, and with all thy might."—Deut. 6: 5.

Promise.

"And the Lord thy God will circumcise thine heart, and the heart of thy seed, to love the Lord thy God with all thine heart, and with all thy soul, that thou mayest live."—Deut. 30:6.

KEPT.

Commands.

"Keep thy heart with all diligence; for out of it are the issues of life."—Prov. 4: 23.

Promises.

"My help cometh from the Lord, which made heaven and earth. He will not suffer thy foot to be moved: he that keepeth

"Keep yourselves in the love of God, looking for the mercy of our Lord Jesus Christ unto eternal life."—Jude 21.

thee will not slumber. Behold, he that keepeth Israel shall neither slumber nor sleep. The Lord is thy keeper: the Lord is thy shade upon thy right hand. The sun shall not smite thee by day, nor the moon by night. The Lord shall preserve thee from all evil: he shall preserve thy soul."—Psa. 121: 2-7.

"Thou wilt keep him in perfect peace, whose mind is stayed on thee: because he trusteth in thee."—Isa. 26: 3.

"And the peace of God, which passeth all understanding, shall keep your hearts and minds through Christ Jesus."—Phil. 4: 7.

"But the Lord is faithful, who shall stablish you, and keep you from evil." —2 Thess. 3: 3.

"Little children, keep yourselves from idols."— 1 John 5: 21.

"Who are kept by the power of God through faith unto salvation ready to be revealed in the last time."—1 Pet. 1: 5.

"Now unto him that is able to keep you from falling, and to present you faultless before the presence of his glory with exceeding joy. To the only wise God our Savior, be glory and majesty, dominion and power, both now and ever. Amen."—Jude 24, 25.

PERFECT OBEDIENCE.

Commands.

"Thou hast commanded us to keep thy precepts diligently."—Psa. 119: 4.

"But this thing commanded I them, saying, Obey my voice, and I will be your God, and ye shall be my people: and walk ye in all the ways that I have commanded you, that it may be well unto you."—Jer. 7: 23.

"We ought to obey God rather than men."—Acts 5: 29.

"If ye love me keep my commandments."—John 14: 15.

"He that hath my commandments, and keepeth them, he it is that loveth me."—John 14:21.

"Teaching them to observe all things whatsoever I have commanded you: and, lo, I am with you alway, even unto the end of the world. Amen."—Matt. 28: 20.

"Let us hear the conclusion of the whole matter: Fear God, and keep his commandments: for this is the whole duty of man."—Eccl. 12: 13.

Promises.

"For this is the love of God, that we keep his commandments: and his commandments are not grievous."—1 Jno. 5: 3.

"For my yoke is easy, and my burden is light."—Matt. 11: 30.

"Elect according to the fore-knowledge of God the Father, through *sanctification of the Spirit, unto obedience*."—1 Pet. 1: 2.

"And I will put my Spirit within you, and cause you to walk in my statutes, and ye shall keep my judgments, and do them."—Eze. 36: 27.

"I will run the way of thy commandments, when thou shalt enlarge my heart."—Psa. 119: 32.

"Our heart is enlarged."—2 Cor. 6: 11.

"Be ye also enlarged."—Verse 13.

WALK EVEN AS HE WALKED.

Commands.	*Promises.*
"Walk before me and be thou perfect."—Gen. 17: 1.	"Righteousness shall go before him; and shall set us in the way of his steps."—Psa. 85: 13.
"For even hereunto were ye called: because Christ also suffered for us, leaving us an example, that ye should follow his steps."—1 Pet. 2: 21.	"The law of God is in his heart; none of his steps shall slide."—Psa. 37: 31.
"He that saith he abideth in him ought himself also so to walk, even as he walked."—1 John 2: 6.	"And what agreement hath the temple of God with idols? for ye are the temple of the living God; as God hath said, I will dwell in them, and walk in them; and I will be their God, and they shall be my people."–2 Cor. 6:16.

Several years ago it occurred to our mind to prepare and preach the Word, thus placing in a balance the commands and promises of God. An abridgment of the lesson we then used found its way into the Bible Readings published by Brothers Kilpatrick and Speck, not, however, to their blame. We speak of this that the reader may know we have not stolen the labors and credit of another. This is a thing we detest, likewise doth God.

Now, beloved reader, what can you say to these scriptures? How can you justify yourself

in being less than perfect in all the moral attributes of God, since you are commanded thus
to be, and every requirement is backed by the
promised grace of God to fulfill it in you?
Should a mother say, "My child, go and wash
your dirty face:" were there no water, or any
other cleansing element provided, nor attain-
able, the little one might truthfully say, "Mother I can't." But when the mother places before
it a bowl of good soft water, soap, wash rag and
towel, and demands of it to wash, all must admit
it will be without excuse if still unclean. And
just so, there is a fountain open to the house of
David, for sin and for uncleanness. Zech. 13: 1.
And pointing to this, God speaks to all sinners,
filthy professors, and unsanctified believers, saying, "Wash you, make you clean." "Cleanse
your hands ye sinners, and purify your hearts
ye double minded." And yet men are foolish
enough to think they have a cloak for their sins
and excuse for their filthiness. Yea, they say,
God commands us to be holy, perfect and pure,
but we cannot wash and remain clean in this
world. Thus they contradict the word of God
and make him a liar, and shall utterly perish in
their unbelief and uncleanness. Reader, as God
is true, *salvation is perfect, and will make you*

perfect, and keep you *blameless* in God's sight, to the coming of the Lord. And if you neglect so GREAT SALVATION you will stand before God in your iniquity, speechless and without a cloak to cover your shame.

————▶•◀————

13th. SALVATION ADAPTED TO EVERY NEED AND CONDITION OF THE SOUL.

The infinite wisdom and actual divinity of the Holy Bible is wonderfully demonstrated in this fact. No other book on earth is both instructive, interesting, and never exhausted; both by ignorant and learned, by youth and mature minds. To such as love God and the truth; and especially to such as have been conformed to the image of his Son, be they profound and cultured, or the most illiterate and simple, the inspired volume is ever precious, unfolding new and rich mines of golden thought at every reading, even down to old age.

How marvelously the inspired volume is adapted to the wants of mankind as a *Book of Salvation.*

Throughout the whole world it has been a fact in human experience, that a sacrifice was needed to atone for the sins of our race. Everywhere the impression rests upon the human heart that God's wrath has been provoked by sin in this world. And in nearly all heathen lands, when the torch of heaven's truth was lifted there, it found men inflicting tortures of some kind upon themselves, or sacrificing in cruel death their own offspring, with a hope of satisfying offended justice. Oh reader, is not the gospel of *God's salvation* glad tidings of great joy to all this sin-stricken world? Does it not exactly meet that deeply and universally felt want in the human breast, of a sacrifice for our sins? How gracious the words of Him who knows and bears the sins and griefs of all our race! How wonderfully they anticipate our inward condition, and announce relief to the oppressed and struggling soul! "Come unto me all ye that labor and are heavy laden, and I will give you rest. Take my yoke upon you and learn of me; for I am meek and lowly in heart: and ye shall find rest unto your souls."—Matt. 11: 28, 29.

Look at all this unhappy world. Are not the hearts of the children of men like the ever restless waters of the sea? Behold the Lamb of God who taketh away our sins; the Prince of peace who calms the sea of inward fear and guilt.

And the infinite wisdom of God has placed this *great salvation* in reach of all. The wise of heart and understanding, if only humble minded, may enter there and find, not only a perfect redemption, but also the wonderful stores of wisdom for which he thirsts. The most simple and unlearned find no difficulty in grasping and appropriating the saving grace of God as soon as they become willing to learn of Him who is meek and lowly in heart.

The wonderful fact in the plan of redemption is this: it heals the malady of sin from the inmost core of our nature. It enters and changes the whole bent of our moral being. It purifies the very fountain of thought and action. It lifts up a perfect standard of holiness, and conforms our affections to the same. It demands a life of absolute freedom from sin, and creates that life in us. "The law made nothing perfect, but the bringing in of a better hope did." "The blood of bulls and of goats, and the ashes of an heifer, sprinkling the unclean, sanctifieth to the purifying of the flesh"—rendered persons outwardly and legally pure. But, "How much more shall—yea, doth—the blood of Christ,

who, through the eternal Spirit, offered himself
without spot to God, purge your conscience from
dead works to serve the living God."—Heb.9:13,
14. Namely, the blood of the new covenant
purges our very nature, and produces an inward
consciousness of purity and moral soundness.

Such a salvation was needed by our fallen
race. After king David had been led by the
tempter to tarnish his beautiful life with one
dark spot of sin, in his humiliation he was led
to deeply scrutinize the human heart, and the
hidden causes of those outcroppings of sin, that
are so opposite to the general character and
principles of righteousness. And, behold! he
discovered that he "was shapen in iniquity; and
in sin did his mother conceive him." By the
sin of our first parents a vein of evil nature has
been transmitted down through all our race.
This he felt the need of having removed. "Behold, thou desirest truth in the inward parts."
To insure a pure stream the fountain must be
cleansed. And he through the Spirit predicted
such a thorough remedy for sin in the following
prayer: "Purge me with hyssop, and I shall
be clean: wash me, and I shall be whiter than
snow." "Create in me a clean heart, O God; and
renew a right spirit within me."—Psa. 51: 5–10.

Time moves on. The Son of God appears to put away sin by the sacrifice of himself; and in response to the heart of man that longs for inward purity we hear him say, "*I will, be thou clean,*" "and the blood of Jesus Christ his Son cleanseth us from all sin," and "all unrighteousness," which includes inbred unrighteousness.

Some ancient philosophers discovered and taught very pure and perfect ethics. But they confessed themselves unable to live up to their own standard, much less impart an ability to their pupils to do so. Jesus our Lord and Savior so far exceeded all other moral philosophers, that he taught the only perfect law ever delivered to man, exemplified it in his life, and has power to raise all his disciples to the same standard. Enabling us not only to walk in a perfect way before God, but to do it easily and naturally. Outward holiness is just as spontaneous in the life, where perfect holiness reigns within, as good fruit naturally adorns a good tree. Oh how shall we thank God for this *new creating salvation in Jesus our Lord*! Let the vilest come to him and realize an entire revolution from sin unto holiness.

Another beautiful fact in the adaptation of

salvation to our needs is this: It does not only impart that grace and fortitude by which men can readily resist all temptations to evil, but its own inward happiness utterly weans the mind and heart from all sinful indulgences. The ransomed soul is so perfectly satiated with its own heavenly feast of love and holy delight, that the allurements of this world become utterly distasteful. All evil is repelled by the surpassing delight of that which is holy and good. How can the base mud-cakes of sinful pleasure, "*the bread of wickedness*," excite desire in a soul that is accustomed to eat "angel's food?" Thus did Nehemiah testify: "The joy of the Lord is my strength."—8: 10. The *joys of salvation* invest the soul with boldness to reject all offered pleasures of sin. Behold the presence of God is with his people. And, "In thy presence is *fulness of joy*; at thy right hand there are pleasures forevermore."—Psa. 16: 11. "Therefore everlasting joy shall be unto them."—Isa. 61: 7. The human heart, it is true, was created for and ardently thirsts after happiness. *Salvation fills that desire, and abundantly satiates that thirst.* FULL SALVATION, and nothing else will do it. "And in this mountain—of his holiness—shall the LORD of hosts make unto all people a feast of fat things, a feast of wines on the lees, of fat things full of marrow, of wines on the lees well refined." "For in this mountain shall the hand of the Lord rest."—Isa. 25: 6, 10.

Oh, if poor sinners but knew that the love of God imparts a "fulness of joy," a perfect delight in all the will of God; and raises us above all relish for the miserable pleasures they are acquainted with in the life of sin, then would they gladly exchange sin for salvation, and the drudgery of Satan for the peaceful service of God.

Again, *salvation* is adapted to the wants of the human soul in its perfect keeping power. The death of Christ atones for our transgression, his resurrection gives us victory over death, and his life is a pledge of our preservation in him. "Because he liveth, we shall live also."

Hence the apostle Jude had the pleasure of writing a letter "to them that are sanctified by God the Father, and preserved in Jesus Christ; and called." And Peter testifies that we "are kept by the power of God through faith unto salvation, ready to be revealed in the last time." —1 Pet. 1: 5.

Many poor souls hesitate to give themselves to God for fear they will not be able to endure unto the end. Oh cast such fears to the winds! God's salvation provides for our eternal preservation from sin, and no child of God ever needs to have the sad experience of a backslider. *The cure of sin is both a thorough and a permanent success.*

In fact the *"salvation that is in Christ Jesus with eternal glory,"* fully and forever provides for every want of the human soul, creating us every whit whole, satisfying all our desires, and preserving us triumphant over sin, and blameless in the sight of God. And the great remedy is so miraculously adapted to man that the most feeble in mind can appreciate its blessings as well as the wise. All responsible men and women, of all nations, and under all circumstances, may come to Christ and be saved, and everlastingly preserved in him, if they will hear his voice and obey.

14th. SALVATION PROVIDES FOR THE HEALING OF THE BODY.

Jesus, the Lamb of God, who bore the sin of the world, also, "Himself took our infirmities, and bare our sicknesses."—Isa. 51: 4, 5. Matt. 8: 16, 17. He is, therefore, a complete Savior of the body from sickness, as well as the soul from sin. "And he healed all that were sick."

"And Jesus went about all Galilee, teaching in their synagogues, and preaching the gospel of the kingdom, and healing all manner of sickness and all manner of disease among the people."—Matt. 4: 23.

"And Jesus went about all the cities and villages, teaching in their synagogues, and preaching the gospel of the kingdom, and healing every sickness and every disease among the people."—Matt. 9: 35.

What a wonderful benefactor to poor suffering humanity! Nor has his love and sympathy grown less by the lapse of centuries, nor his power and willingness to save and heal diminished. In fact he is "Jesus Christ the same yesterday and to day and forever."—Heb. 13: 8. The same gracious power of God that was manifest in healing the sick in the morning of this last dispensation, was designed to bless the church of the living God to the end of time. Hence it was couched in the final commission and sent "into all the world," and "to the end of the world."—Matt. 28: 19, 20. "And he said unto them, 'Go ye into all the world and preach the gospel to every creature. He that believeth

and is baptized shall be saved, but he that be
lieveth not shall be damned. *And these signs
shall follow them that believe. * * * They shall lay
hands on the sick and they shall recover."*—
Mark 16: 17, 18.

These signs did follow the apostles, as the
inspired history shows; and the same miracle-
healing continued to be manifest through the
second and third century, and gradually died
away in the loss of spirituality through the
apostasy. But with the reformation of Bible
holiness it also revived, and in these last days
thousands are being healed of all manner of
diseases. And thousands of poor sinners who
are oppressed with afflictions, and contracting
doctor bills they are scarcely able to pay, would
be made every whit whole without money and
without price, and also without medicine; if
they would give their hearts to God, and their
case in the hands of the Great Physician, who
came to seek and to save the lost, and to heal
the afflicted. He is the living ever present
Physician in all the families of the saints. And
he invites all to cast their burdens upon him.
Oh how great in every way, the blessedness of
having such a Friend, such a Savior, such a
salvation of soul and body!

15th. SALVATION REASONABLE.

Under this head an extensive field of thought is opened up. Every minutia of the system of divine truth might be examined and found in harmony with pure reason. But we can only take space to call attention to a few points.

1. The Incarnation and Suffering of Christ. This exhibition of divine wisdom men and angels could never have conceived. Angels desired to look into the plan by which God would redeem our race (1 Pet. 1:10, 11), but it appears they could not comprehend it until Christ was born in Bethlehem. Then they understood, and with joyful strains sounded the news to earth. Luke 2:9-11. Though human reason could never have given birth to such a plan, it is nevertheless perfectly philosophical.

The laws of a just and unchangeable God had been broken. Death—natural, and spiritual, or separation from God—was the penalty. Both the justice and immutability of God demand the penalty must be executed, either upon the violator of the law, or some one in his stead. Who can offer his life as a ransom for man? God, being a spirit, cannot die. A creature sacrifice would necessarily elicit all the glory;

hence would leave man still unrestored to his original object, namely, to glorify God his Maker. How, then, could man be redeemed? Who but the Infinite could have devised a plan? When a creature sacrifice was insufficient, and the Creator, as a spirit, could not die, the Deity clothes himself with a suffering nature in the person of his Son; put on a mortal body, that he might die on our behalf. "God was manifest in the flesh."—1 Tim. 3: 16. Oh how wonderful! Thus we have a Savior who, "By the grace of God, tasted death for every man."—Heb. 2: 9. "For Christ also hath once suffered for sins, the just for the unjust, that he might bring us to God."—2 Pet. 3: 18. "And that the abundant grace might, through the thanksgiving of many, redound to the glory of God." In short, we have a Savior who came into the physical conditions of man, that we might be well assured of his sympathy and love for us; and who could die in our stead, and thus satisfy the demands of the law and of justice; and yet divine; one with the Father, so that we can render all praise and honor and glory to his name, without detracting from the glory of the Father. Oh the wonders of redeeming wisdom and love!

2. *Salvation is perfectly reasonable in its*

7

conditions. First, it is free. It is God, and "God is love." And "If a man would give all the substance of his house for love, it would utterly be contemned.—Songs 8: 7. Salvation can no more be bought than can love. It is purely the gift of divine love and mercy. And who can find fault with such an overflow of divine goodness? Thousands would purchase salvation at most any price if it could thus be obtained. But that would be incompatible with the Divine Goodness, and also rob him of the glory. It would also leave man an occasion to boast in self, and so be a detriment to him. But salvation is free. So it is available for all men, and God gets all the glory; and justice and reason approve the wondrous plan.

As it cannot be bought by money, so likewise, it is "Not by works of righteousness which we have done, but according to his mercy, he saved us, by the washing of regeneration, and the renewing of the Holy Spirit."—Tit. 3: 5, 6. Good works are excluded from having any part in obtaining salvation, for the same good reasons that money is no consideration.

Repentance is the first condition of salvation. It means a godly sorrow for sin, confessing and forever forsaking sin. To repent is to cease from all sinning in the future. "Repentance is unto life."—Acts 11: 18. "Unto salvation."—2 Cor. 7: 10. It is sure to bring the soul to the point where faith grasps the boon of eternal life. It is the gift of God, to the Jew first, Acts 5: 3, also to the Gentile, Acts 11: 18.

The necessity of repentance arises from man's wrong attitude toward the Creator, and his God-dishonoring deeds of sin. The rebellion of the wicked against the government of God justly provokes his wrath. And man is wholly to blame for the deplorable alienation between him and his Maker. For, though he has striven against the Almighty, blasphemed his holy name, and trampled upon his righteous laws; "Nevertheless he left not himself without witness, in that he did good, and gave us rain from heaven, and fruitful seasons, filling our hearts with food and gladness."—Acts 14: 17.

Therefore it is reasonable that men should repent of their sins. Yea, "The goodness of God leadeth thee to repentance."—Rom. 2: 4. Shame on the man or woman who can breathe the breath God opens his hand of love to give you (Isa. 42: 12. Job 12: 10), walk about upon his beautiful footstool, enjoy the sunbeams that he has created, and live upon his bounties, and

yet live in open sin in his sight! Oh the awful
presumption of sin, the shameful ingratitude of
the sinner! Be astonished, O heavens, at the
wickedness of earth!

A thousand reasons demand repentance of
rebellious mankind. First, the Almighty commands it. John began the good news of the
kingdom of heaven on earth with the cry, "*Repent.*" And "After that John was put in prison,
Jesus came into Galilee, preaching the gospel
of the kingdom of God, and saying, The time is
fulfilled and the kingdom of God is at hand:
repent ye and believe the gospel."–Mark 1:14,15.
Yea, "Except ye repent ye shall all likewise
perish."—Luke 13:3, 5. And when he commissioned his disciples, "They went out, and
preached that men should repent."—Mark 6:12.
Alluding to the ignorance and darkness that
enveloped the earth prior to the coming of
Christ, the faithful apostle to the Gentiles said,
"And the times of this ignorance God winked
at; but now commandeth all men everywhere to
repent: because he hath appointed a day, in the
which he will judge the world in righteousness
by that man whom he hath ordained; whereof
he hath given assurance unto all men, in that he
hath raised him from the dead."—Acts 17:30,31.

God knows that no sinner can stand before his holy presence. Hence, in view of the awful judgment day, he commands all men to repent. And what reason under heaven can men give for not obeying the voice of love and mercy, that only seeks the happiness of mankind?

Again, *faith* is the great condition upon which salvation is suspended. In every way it may be viewed it is perfectly just and reasonable. Man lost the image and favor of God by doubting his word; hence he can only be re-instated by believing the same. Salvation by faith in Christ Jesus is reasonable also, because his truth endureth forever, and it is impossible for him to lie. Can it be said in truth that there is anything difficult or unreasonable in believing Him who is the very embodiment of truth? Is it hard to credit the words of a man who has never lied? Surely not. Then "believe on the Lord Jesus Christ and thou shalt be saved." *Salvation* in all its principles, provisions, conditions and operations, is indeed consonant with the highest claims of reason. Why, then, O sinner, are you not saved?

16th. SALVATION NOW.

"Thus saith the Lord, In an acceptable time have I heard thee, and in a day of salvation have I helped thee; and I will preserve thee." —Isa. 49: 8.

Here is a special day of salvation spoken of, an acceptable time. The most propitious season of God's grace to man. Now where shall we locate this glorious time of deliverance and preservation? Though spoken of in the present tense, it is very evident that it is not to be located in the time of the prophet, which was under the law. Because the entire Old Testament pointed forward to a more gracious dispensation of divine love and mercy in the last days. "Knowing that a man is not justified by the works of the law."—Gal. 2: 16. The law day was not the day of salvation.

* Shall we then look for it in a future time? By some it is referred to an age to come. But the scriptures leave no room for such vague suppositions. Let us look for a positive location of the above prophecy. Read the apostle Paul in 2 Cor. 6: 1, 2. He beseeches the brethren, "That ye receive not the grace of God in vain, For he saith, I have heard thee in a time

accepted, and *in a day of salvation have I suc-coured thee.*" Here the apostle quotes the very thing announced in Isa. 49: 8. And now hear his application of the same. He proceeds, "*Be-hold, now is the accepted time;* BEHOLD, NOW IS THE DAY OF SALVATION." How absolutely clear and conclusive! The great day of salvation is now. Now in the dispensation of the Holy Spirit. This one declaration of divine truth perfectly refutes every theory of a more propi-tious age to come. If, as age-to-come advocates say, a more glorious day of salvation is yet pending, then it is not true that now is pre-em-inently the day of salvation. But, on the other hand, if the apostle testified to the truth, then all teachers of a more perfect salvation in a millennial age to come are false prophets, de-ceived of the devil, and deceiving all who be-lieve their vain imaginations. But the apostle spake by inspiration of God. See 1 Cor. 14: 37. Therefore, it is settled by the voice of Jehovah. "Behold, now is the day of salvation," now the special time singled out in the plan of the Almighty to save all who hear and obey the gospel.

"Wherefore, as the Holy Ghost saith, To day if ye will hear his voice, harden not your hearts."

—Heb. 3: 7, 8. Here again the special time of salvation is defined as to day, and when ye hear the voice of God. That is, all through this gospel era, whenever a soul hears the "Spirit and the bride say, Come," that is the propitious time to escape from sin. And to reject the great boon is to harden the heart.

The above words in Heb. 3: 7, 8, are quoted from Psa. 95: 7–9. But mark what the apostle puts in. "Wherefore, as the Holy Ghost saith, To day," etc. So the Holy Spirit through him applies the to day salvation of the psalmist to the present time. He repeats the quotation in Heb. 3: 15; 4: 7. Now, *to day*, TO DAY, is held out by the divine hand of love and mercy the only hope of this lost world, the last offer of salvation.

When Jesus expired upon the cross, he said, "*It is finished.*" The price of our redemption was fully paid. He went down into the grave and conquered death, "and was raised again for our justification."—Rom. 4: 25. He ascended to heaven in triumph, sent the Holy Spirit to awaken, quicken, and sanctify; and thus execute the perfect salvation he had purchased upon the cross. He commissioned a perpetual living ministry to publish his salvation to "every creature," in all nations to the end of the world. "To declare, I say, *at this time*, his righteousness: that he might be just, and the justifier of him which believeth in Jesus."—Rom. 3: 26.

Nor did he leave a hint in their commission, or anywhere else in his Word, that lays a foundation for any other day of salvation but the present. But through his ministry he gives all men this promise and fair warning: "He that believeth and is baptized shall be saved; but he that believeth not shall be damned."—Mark 16: 16. Thus no opportunity of salvation was ever to be extended to Adam's race beyond the present gospel of Christ.

Accordingly it is a fact clearly recorded that men received salvation now and here. "For the grace of God that bringeth salvation hath appeared to all men, teaching us that, denying ungodliness and worldly lusts, we should live soberly, righteously, and godly, in this present world; looking for that blessed hope, and the glorious appearing of the great God and our Savior Jesus Christ."—Tit. 2: 11–13. This is very plain. The grace of God brings salvation now and here, resulting in a holy life in this present world. While we are only to look for the coming of the great God and our Savior

Jesus Christ in the future, which will be the hour of the resurrection. "For the Lord himself shall descend from heaven with a shout, with the voice of the archangel, and with the trump of God: and the dead in Christ shall rise first: then we which are alive and remain shall be caught up together with them in the clouds, to meet the Lord in the air: and so shall we ever be with the Lord."—1 Thess. 4:16, 17. The same also will be the day of judgment. See Jude 14,15.

"Not by works of righteousness which we have done, but according to his mercy he saved us, by the washing of regeneration, and renewing of the Holy Ghost."—Tit. 3: 5.

"Who hath saved us, and called us with a holy calling, not according to our works, but according to his own purpose and grace, which was given us in Christ Jesus before the world began."—2 Tim. 1: 9.

"By grace ye are saved."—Eph. 2: 5.

"But now being made free from sin, and become servants to God, ye have your fruit unto holiness, and the end everlasting life."-Rom.6:22.

In all these texts we see that salvation had been already attained. So it is a fact that God saves us now. Hence now is the day of salvation in deed and in truth.

17th. SALVATION NOW OR NEVER.

With this great truth stamped upon the hearts of the apostles and early ministers, they made all speed to carry the glad tidings of a perfect, free, and present salvation to all men. And as to the future, it cannot be denied that, with one voice, they pointed to it as only having in store the resurrection of all men, the reward of the righteous, and the banishment of the wicked to hell. All of which was to transpire on the last day of this last dispensation. Thus they followed their Master in holding forth salvation now, and only judgment and eternity to come. Peter testifies that, "Receiving the end of your faith, even the salvation of your souls," we "are kept by the power of God through faith unto salvation, ready to be revealed in the last time." —1 Pet. 1: 5, 9. And furthermore declares that "*The end of all things is at hand;* be ye therefore sober and watch unto prayer."—1 Pet. 3: 7. This language is too plain to be misunderstood. A perfect salvation has prepared us, and does preserve us in condition to be revealed in the last time; and the end of all things is at hand, next to appear. This must include the end of time, the end of probation, the end of the world,

the end of the redemptive reign of Christ. As
Paul says, "He must reign till he hath put all
enemies under his feet." And, speaking of the
resurrection of them "that are Christ's at his
coming," he adds, "*Then cometh the end*, when he
shall have delivered up the kingdom to God,
even the Father."—1 Cor. 15:23-25. "*Cometh*" is
not in the text. "Then, the end," is the correct
rendering. Christ's reign is upon a mediatorial
throne. The instant he leaves that throne, the
world will be without an advocate, without a
Savior, or further opportunity of salvation.
Yea, "The end of all things is at hand," and
salvation is now or never.

But we will hear Peter a little further. Read
his loud blasts of warning in 2 Pet. 3. "But the
heavens and the earth, which are now, by the
same word are kept in store, reserved unto fire
against the day of judgment and perdition of
ungodly men."—Ver. 7. That day of fire which
shall consume this world, "the day of judgment
and perdition of ungodly men," will be the day
of the Lord's second advent. See verse 4. "But
the day of the Lord will come as a thief in the
night; in the which the heavens—atmosphere—
shall pass away with a great noise, and the elements shall melt with fervent heat, the earth

also, and the works that are therein, shall be burned up."—Ver. 10. So we see clearly that the end of all things does not mean a renovation of this earth; but an utter consuming, and melting of the same into the same chaotic state its matter existed before the six days of creation. In this chapter the coming of Christ, the day of judgment, and utter destruction of the earth and its works, are all pointed forward to as the events of one great and last "*day of God,* wherein the heavens—the atmosphere—being on fire shall be dissolved, and the elements—that compose the earth—shall melt with ferventheat."—Ver.12.

Now let us see if any offers of salvation to our race will extend beyond that awful day. Owing to the long pending of Christ's second advent, it was foreseen that "There shall come in the last days scoffers, walking after their own lusts, and saying, Where is the promise of his coming?" Wherefore the Lord, by this inspired writer, explains the reason of his delay. "The Lord is not slack concerning his promise, as some men count slackness; but is longsuffering to us-ward, not willing that any should perish, but that all should come to repentance."—V. 9.

"And account that the longsuffering of our Lord is salvation."—Ver. 15.

Surely this is all very plain. The long pending of Christ's second advent, we are told, is not
because of any slackness on the part of the Lord
to fulfill his promise, but because he is not willing that poor sinners should be cut off from all
hope and eternally perish. We are, therefore,
taught to count the longsuffering, the pro-
longed delay of the Lord, and day of judgment,
"is salvation." So let all men take warning that
"*salvation*" is now, and only now; is all on this
side of the coming of the Lord. Is it not one
of the most astonishing things that devils ever
invented on earth, that men—such for instance
as Russell, the age-to-come heretic—can be so
subverted as to teach that now is not the time
of salvation and healing, but that glorious work
is "deferred until after Christ's second advent,
in the millennial age?" How dare men teach
such shocking lies in the face of God's word?
Truth declares that now is the day of salvation,
and that the present day of grace is drawn out
by the mercy of God, to enable more lost sinners to be saved; and that when Christ comes
salvation work will forever cease, the judgment
and perdition of all the wicked take place, and
this earth perish. Whereas, Russell asserts that
now is not yet the day of salvation, but it will

be ushered in by the second advent. Oh reader, *"let God be true and every man a liar,"* who wickedly disputes his Word!

Let us now listen to some further testimony from the apostle Paul. "Neither let us tempt Christ, as some of them also tempted, and were destroyed of serpents. Neither murmur ye, as some of them also murmured, and were destroyed of the destroyer. Now all these things happened unto them for ensamples: and they are written for our admonition, upon whom the ends of the world are come."—1 Cor. 10: 9–11.

How solemn this declaration! God has from the beginning meted out and fixed the time of this planet's end. One long age has succeeded another, until we have entered the *"last days"* of this world's career. Upon us, in the present dispensation, the ends of the world have fallen. And we have approached eighteen hundred years nearer that final end than the apostle lived; and here we stand upon the very verge of eternity. Just a small step before us has fallen the end of the world. Oh how much more weighty the exhortation of Peter falls upon us than upon the church when first written! "Seeing then that all these things shall be dissolved, what manner of persons ought ye to be in all holy conversation and godliness?" "Wherefore, beloved, seeing that ye look for such things, be diligent that ye may be found of him in peace, without spot, and blameless." —2 Pet. 3: 11, 14.

Eternal happiness or woe turns upon the condition in which death, or the coming of Christ finds us.

"But this is that which was spoken by the prophet Joel; And it shall come to pass in the last days, saith God, I will pour out of my Spirit upon all flesh: and your sons and your daughters shall prophesy, and your young men shall see visions, and your old men shall dream dreams."—Acts 2: 16, 17.

The last days of this world began with the present Holy Spirit dispensation. "And it shall come to pass—in these last days—that whosoever shall call upon the Lord shall be saved."—Ver. 21. The last time is here, and salvation is now or never.

"But now, once in the end of the world hath he appeared to put away sin by the sacrifice of himself."—Heb. 9: 26. Thus it is rendered in Young's translation: *"Now once, at the full end of the ages."* So the sacrifice of Christ for the sins of the world was at the beginning of the last dispensation, the full end of the ages; and nothing more but eternity is before us. Thus, the Emphatic Diaglott renders, "*But now once for all, at the completion of the ages.*" So the present gospel age is the consummation of all time, the completion of all the ages allotted to this world. Hence, the supposed millennium age is a delusion of the adversary of souls. But now is the day of salvation, *now or never.*

The same fact is announced in 1 Pet. 1:20. "Who verily was foreordained before the foundation of the world, but was manifest in these last times for you."—1 Pet. 1:20.

Here again we must conclude that if these be the "last times," there will be no time for any future salvation. But time and salvation will end with the present gospel era.

We conclude with a very positive testimony of John, the beloved apostle.

"And the world passeth away, and the lust thereof: but he that doeth the will of God abideth forever. Little children, it is the last time: and as ye have heard that antichrist shall come, even now are there many antichrists; whereby we know that it is the last time."—1 John 2:17, 18.

As probation ends with time, and salvation

with probation; and the inspired apostle positively declared that he knew this is the last
time; it follows, as an absolute certainty, that
right now, under the abounding grace of God,
our race is enjoying its last chance of salvation;
and this world is moving through its last epoch
of time. Therefore, behold, now, yea, *now*, is
the day of salvation. Now, O lost sinner, be
saved. It must be NOW OR NEVER.

SALVATION.

Salvation is the sweetest thing
　　That mortal ever found;
My soul can never cease to sing,
　　Such love and peace abound.

REFRAIN:
　Jesus our Friend and Redeemer!
　Jesus, my wonderful light!
Saved by thy grace, we're forever
　Singing the blood that makes me white.

Salvation is omnipotence,
　　Combined with love supreme,
Come down in pity, so intense,
　　To rescue and redeem.

Salvation flows from Father's heart,
　　A stream of holy love;
It floods me all with glory bright,
　　And wings my soul above.

Salvation is a perfect plan;
　　It heals the saddest case
Of all who seek the Son of Man,
　　And find his boundless grace.

Salvation! oh, that word so great!
　　It thrills my heart with joy;
To me it is a rich estate,
　　No foe can e'er destroy.

INDEX.

THE GOSPEL TRUMPET.

Subscription, per yr., $1.00;   Six mo., 50c.
   Three mo., 25c.   Sample copies FREE.

An eight-page Weekly Religious Journal, thoroughly up-to-date in its teaching, unsectarian and uncompromising. Its object is to present the whole gospel in its purity as taught in apostolic times. It opposes all forms of division among Christians, and teaches the oneness of God's people.

THE SHINING LIGHT.

Subscription, one year, 25c.

It contains beautiful Bible stories, gems of poetry and interesting articles on various subjects which both please and instruct the children. Each issue is illustrated with beautiful pictures which enable its little readers to form correct ideas of the subjects represented. It also contains testimonies of full salvation and divine healing. Published weekly.

SUBSCRIPTION RATES TO SUNDAY-SCHOOLS.

Ten copies, three months, (to one address)   - $ .50
Twenty-five copies, three months, (to one address) 1.15
Fifty copies, three months, (to one address)   2.00

DIE EVANGELIUMS POSAUNE.

Subscription, one yr., $1.00; Three mo., 25c.

A Four-page Semi-monthly Religious Journal published in German. It is similar in its teaching to THE GOSPEL TRUMPET, both presenting the doctrine of full salvation of both soul and body.

THE SECRET OF SALVATION:
HOW TO GET IT, AND
HOW TO KEEP IT.
——BY E. E. BYRUM.——

400 Pages.   **Illustrated.**

A book consisting of 111 chapters, every one of which is full of interest and instruction. Christians are shown how to attain to a life of holiness and enjoy a close walk with God. Sinners are instructed how they may be saved from all their sins, evil habits, appetites, and desires, and be made free. The sick are informed how to be healed without medicine.

Beautifully Bound in Cloth, Stamped in Gilt, – **$1.00.**
In Strong Paper Cover,   –   –   –   –   **35c.**

LETTERS OF LOVE AND COUNSEL
FOR "OUR GIRLS."
——By JENNIE C. RUTTY.——

This book is written by a Christian mother and contains wise and wholesome counsel, such as every girl needs to assist her to live a pure and upright life. Beautiful cloth binding.

Price, **$1.00.** – – – – – Paper cover, **35c.**

MOTHERS' COUNSEL ❧ ❧
❧ ❧ TO THEIR SONS.
——BY JENNIE C. RUTTY.——

A very precious volume written expressly for boys and young men. It contains such wise and wholesome counsel as can only flow from the pen of a Christian mother. Boys, young men, you all need this book. If you read it carefully and heed its instructions it may save you much trouble, sorrow, and suffering. Beautifully bound in cloth. Contains about 425 pages.

Price, postpaid,   –   –   –   –   –   **$1.00.**